THE POWER OF GOD

Romans

NELSON
IMPACT™
Bible Study Series

THE POWER OF GOD

Romans

NELSON IMPACT
A Division of Thomas Nelson Publishers
Since 1798

www.thomasnelson.com

Published by Nelson Impact, a Division of Thomas Nelson, Inc., P.O. Box 141000, Nashville, Tennessee, 37214.

Printed in the United States of America.

05 06 07 – 9 8 7 6 5 4 3 2 1

A Word from the Publisher…

Be diligent to present yourself approved to God, a worker who does not need to be ashamed, rightly dividing the word of truth.

2 Timothy 2:15 NKJV

We are so glad that you have chosen this study guide to enrich your biblical knowledge and strengthen your walk with God. Inside you will find great information that will deepen your understanding and knowledge of this book of the Bible.

Many tools are included to aid you in your study, including ancient and present-day maps of the Middle East, as well as timelines and charts to help you understand when the book was written and why. You will also benefit from sidebars placed strategically throughout this study guide, designed to give you expanded knowledge of language, theology, culture, and other details regarding the Scripture being studied.

We consider it a joy and a ministry to serve you and teach you through these study guides. May your heart be blessed, your mind expanded, and your spirit lifted as you walk through God's Word.

Blessings,

Edward (Les) Middleton, M. Div.
Editor-in-Chief, Nelson Impact

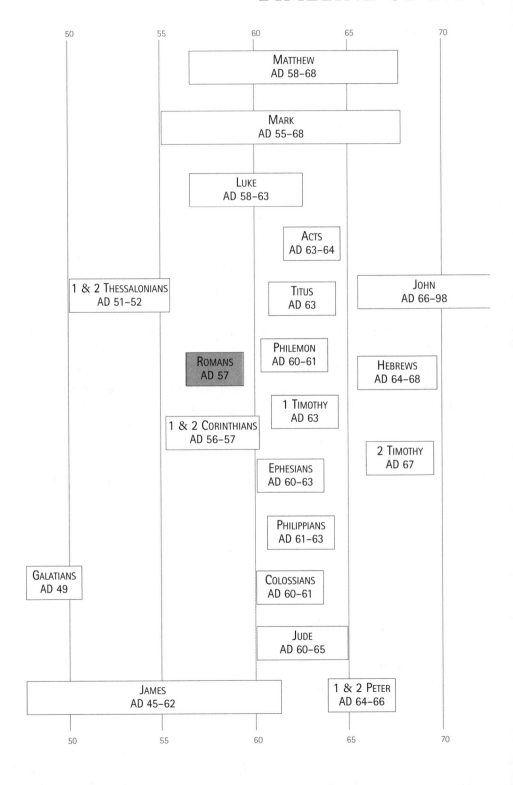

50   55   60   65   70

MATTHEW
AD 58–68

MARK
AD 55–68

LUKE
AD 58–63

ACTS
AD 63–64

1 & 2 THESSALONIANS
AD 51–52

TITUS
AD 63

JOHN
AD 66–98

PHILEMON
AD 60–61

ROMANS
AD 57

HEBREWS
AD 64–68

1 TIMOTHY
AD 63

1 & 2 CORINTHIANS
AD 56–57

2 TIMOTHY
AD 67

EPHESIANS
AD 60–63

PHILIPPIANS
AD 61–63

GALATIANS
AD 49

COLOSSIANS
AD 60–61

JUDE
AD 60–65

JAMES
AD 45–62

1 & 2 PETER
AD 64–66

50   55   60   65   70

TESTAMENT WRITINGS

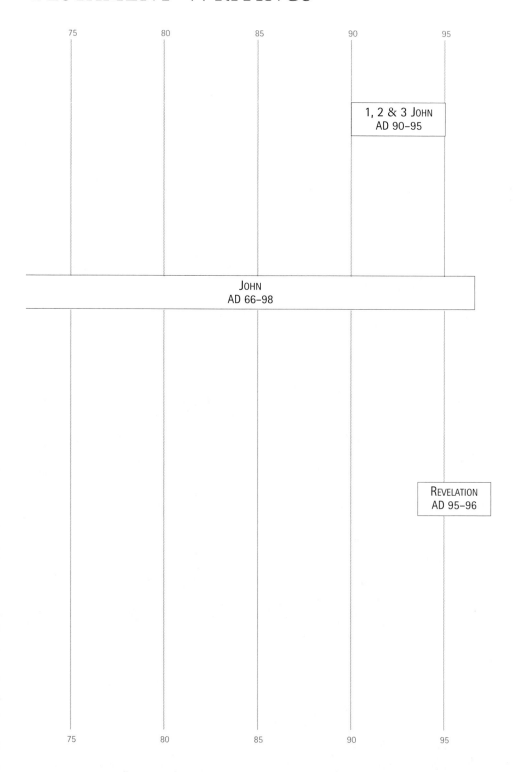

| 75 | 80 | 85 | 90 | 95 |

1, 2 & 3 JOHN
AD 90–95

JOHN
AD 66–98

REVELATION
AD 95–96

| 75 | 80 | 85 | 90 | 95 |

OLD MIDDLE EAST

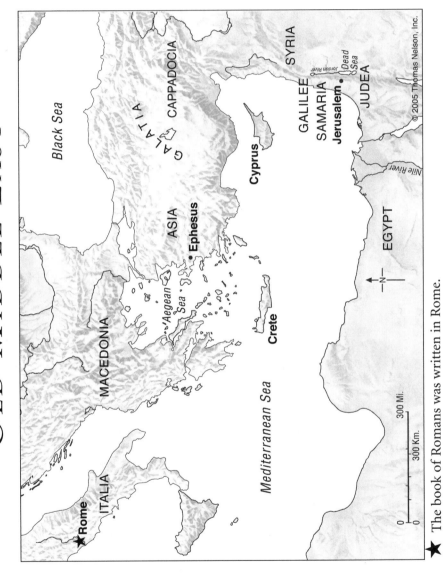

★ The book of Romans was written in Rome.

© 2005 Thomas Nelson, Inc.

MIDDLE EAST OF TODAY

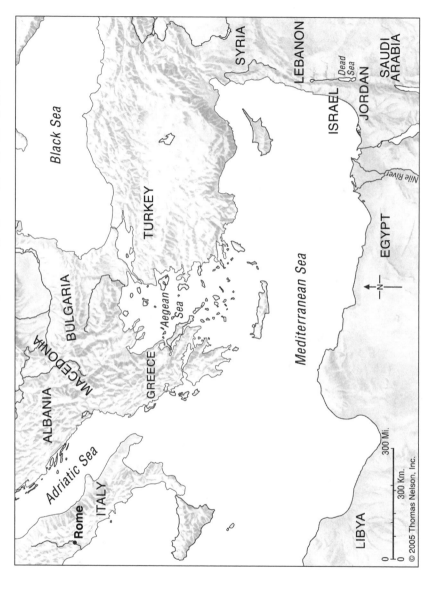

© 2005 Thomas Nelson, Inc.

OLD TESTAMENT DIVISIONS

The Pentateuch
Genesis
Exodus
Leviticus
Numbers
Deuteronomy

Wisdom Literature
Job
Psalms
Proverbs
Ecclesiastes
Song of Solomon

The Historical Books
Joshua
Judges
Ruth
1 Samuel
2 Samuel
1 Kings
2 Kings
1 Chronicles
2 Chronicles
Ezra
Nehemiah
Esther

The Prophetic Books
Isaiah
Jeremiah
Lamentations
Ezekiel
Daniel
Hosea
Joel
Amos
Obadiah
Jonah
Micah
Nahum
Habakkuk
Zephaniah
Haggai
Zechariah
Malachi

NEW TESTAMENT DIVISIONS

The Four Gospels
Matthew
Mark
Luke
John

History
Acts

The Epistles of Paul
Romans
1 Corinthians
2 Corinthians
Galatians
Ephesians
Philippians
Colossians
1 Thessalonians
2 Thessalonians
1 Timothy
2 Timothy
Titus
Philemon

The General Epistles
Hebrews
James
1 Peter
2 Peter
1 John
2 John
3 John
Jude

Apocalyptic Literature
Revelation

ICON KEY

Throughout this study guide, you will find many icon sidebars that will aid and enrich your study of this book of the Bible. To help you identify what these icons represent, please refer to the key below.

BIBLICAL GRAB BAG

A biblical grab bag full of interesting facts and tidbits.

BIBLE

Further exploration of biblical principles and interpretations, along with a little food for thought.

LANGUAGE

Word usages, definitions, interpretations, and information on the Greek and Hebrew languages.

CULTURE

Customs, traditions, and lifestyle practices in biblical times.

ARCHAEOLOGICAL

Archaeological discoveries and artifacts that relate to biblical life, as well as modern-day discoveries.

CONTENTS

INTRODUCTION

The apostle Paul's letter to the Romans, probably written in 57 or 58 AD, has often been called the finest example of its kind in the history of the ancient world. The expression "of its kind," of course, refers to "epistle" in the Greek language, or to "letter" in the English language. For even though the book of Romans has also been called one of the greatest dissertations on fundamental Christian doctrine ever written, it wasn't conceived and created as an abstract doctrinal statement to be published in a book, a newspaper, or a magazine.

It was a *personal letter,* sent by a passionate, brilliant, highly-educated, sometimes physically afflicted, in-your-face kind of man who knew beyond doubt that God had given him a sacred duty to instruct the letter's recipients in matters of faith and doctrine.

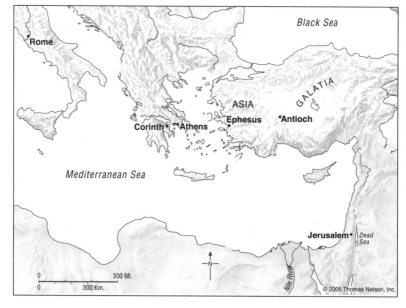

WHO WERE THE ROMAN RECIPIENTS?

In Romans 1:7, Paul addressed his letter "To all who are in Rome, beloved of God, called to be saints" (NKJV). Contrary to what he often did elsewhere, Paul did not address this letter to any one person or any one congregation known to be meeting in any one place. Thus, some scholars believe that Paul's letter to the Romans could have been read aloud (for a public reading is how most of its recipients would have learned its contents) to more than one group of people, while other scholars favor a "one congregation only" scenario.

Either way, who were these "unidentified people"? Undoubtedly, the faith (biblical Judaism) of many of its first hearers had just been revamped and renewed by the life and death of the man they considered their long-promised Messiah, Jesus Christ. At the same time, the letter's main subject might have been quite new to some of the people to whom it was read.

In other words, those who first heard Paul's letter probably included many Jews who had recognized and accepted Christ as their Messiah—*Yeshua*, as they knew Him in Hebrew. But their ranks were being supplemented—more and more every day—by Gentiles (i.e., non-Jews) who were beginning to believe in Jesus Christ with equal fervency. Yet many of these new converts knew next to nothing of the Jewish faith, history, culture, and customs in which the rest of those in the congregation (and Christ Himself, of course) had grown up. Indeed, the paganism of Rome might have been the only background, in matters of faith and doctrine, that some of those who first heard Paul's letter to the Romans had ever really had.

Imagine the "learning gap" Paul had to be addressing! Plus, many of the Romans who first heard Paul's letter also included Jews who did *not* believe that Christ was their Messiah.

So what is the "net" of all this? Well, no one can say with any certainty the number of Gentile believers, Jewish believers, and Jewish non-believers who first heard Paul's letter. Yet despite their diversity, Paul clearly intended to help *all* of the Romans understand how the teachings of Christ could change their lives, no matter where they were starting from.

Wow! What a job! And Paul did it beautifully. What Paul considered his sacred duty has long-since been recognized, by millions of people, as a sacred contribution to the religious heritage of the world.

Which, of course, is why the book of Romans stands head and shoulders above all the rest of the letters of the ancient world. In a word, everything else wound up in second place.

WHO WAS PAUL, ANYWAY?

Most people know the story of Saul, the relentless persecutor of early Christians. Saul himself dramatically embraced that same belief in Christ as the Jewish Messiah on his way to Damascus one day—to persecute more of those pesky believers! (If you are not already familiar with this story, it might be good to fill in the gaps by reading the ninth chapter of Acts.)

How and when Saul's name got changed to *Paul*, in English translations of the Greek New Testament text, is somewhat less certain. He was known by his given name, Saul (*Sha'ul* in Hebrew, the same name as Israel's first king), until Acts 13:9, at which point Luke, the author of Acts, spoke of "Saul, who also is called Paul" (NKJV). From that point forward, except for three times when Paul tells his own story and refers to his being called *Saul* by Christ Himself (in the 22nd and 26th chapters of Acts), he was known in almost all our English translations of the Bible as *Paul*.

3

No matter what name we use, Paul was still a Jew until the day he died as a martyr, most likely in Rome several years after he sent his letter to the Romans. As such, perhaps he can best be described in his own words:

> *If anyone else thinks he may have confidence in the flesh, I more so: circumcised the eighth day, of the stock of Israel, of the tribe of Benjamin, a Hebrew of the Hebrews; concerning the law, a Pharisee; zeal, persecuting the church; concerning the righteousness which is in the law, blameless.(Phil. 3:4–6 NKJV)*

The above quotation comes from a letter to the congregation at Philippi. Paul probably wrote this letter three or four years after his letter to the Romans. It has become one of Paul's more familiar statements about his own ancestry and training. He also saw fit to make one of its main points in Romans 11:1:

> *I say then, has God cast away His people? Certainly not! For I also am an Israelite, of the seed of Abraham, of the tribe of Benjamin. (NKJV)*

In these two quotations, Paul was essentially saying that, if anyone else had a right to brag about his ancestry and his qualifications as a highly trained Jew of the educated class, Paul certainly had the right to brag on his own behalf. Paul was a well-respected rabbi (teacher), trained "at the feet of Gamaliel" (Acts 22:3). Gamaliel (also spelled *Gamliel*), in turn, was the grandson of one of the best-known Pharisaic teachers of all time, a man known as Rabbi Hillel (60 BC–AD 20). Hillel was the first to write down the seven rules of scriptural interpretation, from the ancient Hebrew viewpoint, that are still in wide usage today—rules of logic and orderly presentation that Christ Himself often followed in His own parables and teachings. Paul followed them also in his writings.

WHY CIRCUMCISION ON THE EIGHTH DAY?

God instructed the ancient Jews to circumcise their male babies on the eighth day after birth, as Paul said was done to him. But why eight days? Why not three, or five, or thirty-seven? Modern medical science tells us that, in the vast majority of cases—even as the eyes do not see perfectly when a baby is first born—the blood of a newborn child is not fully able to coagulate and stop unlimited bleeding until the baby is eight days old. So, it's very possible that, without any modern, supplemental means to stop his bleeding, a male child circumcised too soon could have bled to death.

Paul's status as a rabbi is what qualified him to go into the temple and the synagogues, wherever he traveled, to teach and to engage other rabbis in passionate discourse. He kept himself under the authority of the Jewish leaders until a point near the end of his life, when he exercised his right to be tried as a Roman citizen (Acts 22:27, et al). Indeed, he was even given thirty-nine lashes by the Sanhedrin (the Jewish judicial and administrative authorities) on more than one occasion (2 Cor. 6:3–10; Acts 21:21–26; 32), something that never could have happened had he not been a Jew—for the Jews could legally punish only their own.

Also, in that time and place, Paul was probably known as something of a *gaon*, a Hebrew word that meant "Torah genius." In Paul's era, anyone worthy to be called a *gaon* had most likely committed the entire Old Testament to memory, in some cases by using the ancient Hebrew practice of setting the text to a long series of short melodies and thus memorizing it musically. Or, by speaking or declaiming it out loud, many times over, in an open field where no one else could interrupt. (Incidentally, this memorization practice is still used in Arab countries today.)

In short, when Paul called himself "a Hebrew of the Hebrews," in addition to his ancestry he meant that he was intimately familiar with the teachings of biblical Judaism of his day. Thus he certainly knew how those teachings could have expanded and "opened up" to incorporate the message of Jesus Christ. Unfortunately, the leaders of biblical Judaism—and most of the people they led—simply were not willing to listen.

ROME AND RELIGION IN THE FIRST CENTURY

By the time Paul wrote the book of Romans, the Nation of Israel (i.e., Judea and Samaria) had been part of the Roman Empire for a number of years. However, largely because of their strong national identity and their own robust legal code, the Jews had been given several rare privileges within the Roman Empire itself since the time of Julius Caesar. These included:

The right to govern and tax themselves,

The right to establish and enforce their own codes of discipline, to a point just shy of the right to carry out their own executions,

The right to enjoy common meals,

The right to hold real property,

The right of exemption from service in the Roman military machine,

The right not to worship the Roman Emperor, and

The right to assemble together in orderly meetings, on their own schedules.

Perhaps the most significant benefit of all—and closely linked to the Jews' right to gather together—was that Judaism was the only non-pagan religion allowed within the Roman Empire. Partly for this reason, most new believers in Christ, for several years after Christ's death, met in the synagogues with "regular" Jews. The Jews retained this privilege because Judaism had been well-established when the Romans conquered Israel. Perhaps the civilizing influence of Judaism seemed like a secure source and the Romans considered them safe, non-rebellious citizens.

In other words, by letting the Jews be Jews, the Romans apparently felt secure in believing that the Jews would never be a serious threat to the sovereignty of Roman authority. Unfortunately, in AD 70, forty years after the crucifixion of Jesus Christ, they were proven wrong. But Paul did not live to see either the Jewish uprising or the resulting destruction of the temple—plus the expulsion of all Jews from Jerusalem— that were finalized in that year.

At the same time, absolutely no new religions were allowed by the Romans in the years leading up to AD 70. This, in fact, partially explains why the early Christian church eventually had to go underground, into the catacombs, to survive the wanton persecutions of that era, once it began to split off from established Judaism and could no longer find shelter under Judaism's protective umbrella. Indeed, after the destruction of the temple and the expulsion of the Jews, those followers of "The Way" (an earlier name for the sect within Judaism that became Christianity), who stayed on in Jerusalem, no longer had any such umbrella to hide under at all! They were no longer part of a protected or "allowed" religion—indeed, all known Jews had been forbidden to live in Jerusalem—and thus the early believers in Christ dared not openly identify themselves as Jewish in any way—or even as Jewish sympathizers.

Given all this, it still seems very likely that Paul would have been surprised at the persecution of Christians by the Romans that eventually came about. On the contrary, Paul did not expect a brand new religion to emerge from the Judaism he knew so well (see "What Was 'Biblical Judaism'?"). What he

What Was "Biblical Judaism"?

Understanding the difference between what many scholars call "biblical" and "rabbinic" (or "orthodox") Judaism—and why that particular evolution came about—can be very helpful to a proper understanding of the split between Judaism and Christianity that also came about at roughly the same time. The Judaism/Christianity split was not really complete until many years after Paul died, and he probably would have been appalled to see it happen, for that was never his understanding of what God wanted.

Nonetheless, after the Jewish temple in Jerusalem was destroyed by the Romans in AD 70, the several sects of mainstream Judaism that rejected Christ as their Messiah (i.e., the Sadducees, the Pharisees, the Essenes, et al), having no sacred temple and thus no means to perpetuate their sacrificial system, had nowhere to go. Biblical Judaism's prior understanding of how God interacted with humanity—through the righteousness He offered via belief and trust in Him, and the forgiveness of sin He offered via daily sacrifices—was simply left without an anchor.

Thus what we know as "biblical Judaism," a faith whose fundamental rituals could no longer be performed, evolved into "rabbinic" or "orthodox" Judaism. Gradually, orthodox Judaism became a faith based less and less on what had defined it for all the previous centuries, and more and more on what it could still manage to observe of the commandments and guidelines God had given it originally—as now defined and expanded upon by its own rabbis and commentators. This development was accompanied by more and more "pulling into itself" in survival mode, and by its increasing dependence on sincerely pursued "works" that its adherents hoped the God of Creation would accept in place of the blood sacrifices that originally atoned for their sin.

The split between Judaism and Christianity, which came about at roughly the same time was thus a natural split, based on a "Christ–YES!" or "Christ–NO!" dynamic. By that mechanism, Christianity became a defined and structured belief system based on acceptance of Jesus as the divine Son of God, whose sacrifice on the Cross created the grace by which believers could be forgiven of their sin.

Judaism then became an equally defined and structured belief in the God of Creation without acknowledging and accepting Jesus Christ as His divine Son or the mitigating grace of Christ's sacrifice. Unfortunately, the difficulty that Judaism now faced was that it found itself without any viable means of obeying its own sacrificial laws and receiving God's grace—and therefore it evolved in a different direction entirely, by eventually equating "grace" with "works" and thus becoming "rabbinical" rather than "biblical."

After all, Christ predicted the destruction of the temple (basically saying, "You know, you can't hang your whole religion on this temple because it'll soon be knocked down!"), and God allowed all the rest. In the final analysis, only God knows how He will work things out to fulfill the magnificent promises that He gave to the Jews so many years ago. But fulfill them He will, for no one has ever been able to prove that God will ever be anything less than 100 percent faithful to His Word.

hoped would become known as a glorious fulfillment of prophecy, and an enthusiastic acceptance of Jesus Christ as the Jewish Messiah, segued into far more radical and extensive changes than Paul—the ultimate Jew—could possibly have anticipated.

PURPOSE AND THEMES

Within the above context, at a time when so many truly momentous changes were either already in the works or barely a decade away, Paul appears to have had three main purposes for writing his letter to the Romans.

1. He wanted to let the Roman congregation(s) know that he planned to visit them soon.

2. He wanted to provide them with a complete statement of the gospel message, as he believed the Holy Spirit (and those who had known Christ personally, which did not include Paul) had given it to him.

3. He wanted to establish once for all that both Jews and Gentiles alike "are all under sin" (Rom. 3:9), and that all can be saved by faith in God through the person of Jesus Christ. Thus Christ's sacrifice of Himself on the Cross had not changed the means by which men and women could come to belief in God by faith, but had forever changed the means by which their continuing sins could be propitiated before God (the means by which their sins could be forgiven and effectively rendered as non-existent so that God could consider them righteous in His sight, on a continuing basis.)

The main theme of the book of Romans grows out of all the above. In a larger sense, it is the gospel of salvation through Christ. However, in a more specific sense, the theme of Romans involves the fundamental set of understandings on which Christianity rests. These include the understandings that . . .

1. God Himself is holy and righteous in every possible way.

2. In order to stand before God and be recognized by Him, in any capacity whatsoever, we must be righteous as well.

3. God, therefore, imputes righteousness to us through His grace, which was brought about by the sacrifice of His divine Son, Jesus Christ, on the Cross.

Or, if you prefer to say that God extended His grace to sinners through the sacrificial system as well, in prior times, then in number three above, it would be more accurate to say that His grace was not "brought about" but, instead, was suddenly made available in a brand new way by the for-all-time sacrifice of Jesus Christ.

SALVATION THEN AND NOW

Finally, let us add a few additional words of background explanation. Some parts of Romans can be difficult to follow if we do not consider the differences between the words *law* and *grace*, both as those two terms were understood by Paul and the believers in Rome of his time, and as they are sometimes understood by modern believers. In truth, this is a huge subject and goes well beyond the scope of this study guide, but it simply is not possible to study Romans without at least a short discussion—however inadequate it might be—of these such terms, because they will definitely be coming up repeatedly.

So . . . here are some basic concepts to keep in mind as you study Romans.

1. In ancient times, those who were "righteous before God" (in modern times we would call them "saved") were first required to have faith in God just as Christians are today. But—and here's where we encounter the main difference— as an outward expression of their inner spirit of repentance

(and in the firsthand knowledge that the cost of sin is death), they were then required to sacrifice animals to obtain continuing forgiveness of their continuing sins, inevitable because of their human, sinful nature. This is how David could be called righteous (and, indeed, could be one of God's favorites!) even though he sinned more than once, and even though Christ had not yet died for those sins. When the sacrifices made by righteous Jews of that era were offered in the right spirit, the combination of "relationship + sacrifice" kept them righteous in God's eyes, and thus permitted them to have ongoing relationships with Him.

WHAT DID KING DAVID HAVE TO SAY ABOUT SALVATION?

The psalms of King David are a rich source of both inspiration and information about the world David lived in. Psalm 51 is especially helpful in clarifying what we have talked about in this introduction—the differences and the similarities between how God dealt with sin "under the law" and how He now deals with it "under grace." In the passage below, David makes it clear that God accepted sacrifices only when they were offered in the right spirit, from what David calls "a broken and a contrite heart."

O Lord, open my lips,
And my mouth shall show forth Your praise.
For You do not desire sacrifice, or else I would give it;
You do not delight in burnt offering.
The sacrifices of God are a broken spirit,
A broken and a contrite heart—
These, O God, You will not despise.
Do good in Your good pleasure to Zion;
Build the walls of Jerusalem.
Then You shall be pleased with the sacrifices of righteousness,
With burnt offering and whole burnt offering;
Then they shall offer bulls on Your altar.
(Ps. 51:15–19 NKJV, emphasis added).

Conversely, God made it very clear any number of times, in the Scriptures, that sacrifices offered in the wrong spirit, by those who were simply trying to do what they felt was legally required, were wholly unacceptable to Him.

2. Since the death of Christ on the Cross, those who are "saved of God" (the ancient believers might have called such people "righteous before God") have first been required to have faith in God just as believers were before. But we are then given what modern believers call the "free gift of God's grace." Under this grace we are not required by law to make daily sacrifices to atone for our continuing sins but are allowed to accept Christ's sacrifice on our behalf in place of those daily sacrifices.

3. Thus, the only real difference in what we call "salvation" between ancient times and modern times, is the mechanism by which continuing sin, both ours and theirs, was and is forgiven on a continuing basis. To identify this difference one final time in the simplest possible terms:

The ancient Jews were required to sacrifice animals, every day, to cover their sins and achieve what God was willing to accept as righteousness in His eyes. In contrast, for modern Christians, Christ's sacrifice on the Cross has achieved the same result, once and for all.

This means that people from ALL eras can be (and were) saved by God's willingness to absolve us from sin, in His eyes, so we could have a relationship with Him. The only real difference lies in the mechanism by which all such sins—in both the pre-Christ and post-Christ eras, could be overlooked by God.

4. Now . . . all of this is preliminary to the main point of this discussion, which is actually easier to explain than what we've talked about so far!

The "law" that Paul mentioned so often was not exactly what some modern Christians seem to equate with that word. But any such confusion is understandable, because—unfortunately—English does not have a common word, comprehensible to everyone, that equates perfectly to the word *Torah*. *Torah* comes from Hebrew and is the root word for the Greek word that we translate as "law" in most of its occurrences in the New Testament.

In other words, by the time we get to the English word *law*, we are two languages removed from the sense of the original word. So, it can be very helpful to remember that *Torah*, which all the major English translations of the Bible translate as "law," was not "law" as in "Do this (and don't do that) or you go to jail."

On the contrary, *Torah* included everything in the first five books of the Bible, but those first five books are not simply a collection of legal requirements and stipulations. They included a lot of history as well.

At the same time, the portion of *Torah* so often called "the law" contains a total of 613 *mitzvot*, which is a Hebrew word whose true meaning is a lot closer to "guidelines and instructions for righteous living" than it is to "law." How did the *mitzvot* relate to salvation? Not at all!

Thus we encounter one of the most fascinating ironies of modern Christianity, in which we sometimes hear well-meaning Christians say they are "not under the law" yet they still righteously observe the Ten Commandments. Or, they say they are "not under the law" yet they live and participate proudly in a culture which, for countless generations, has taught any number of *Torah's mitzvot*—meaning its guidelines for righteous living—to its children. Many of these are the fundamental rules of Western civilization, under which they live their daily lives even as they claim not to be under any such law.

Here's a simple example from *Torah,* which also occurs (of course) in exactly the same words in exactly the same chapter and verse in the Christian Bible:

> *You shall rise before the gray headed and honor the presence of an old man, and fear your God: I am the* LORD. *(Lev. 19:32 NKJV)*

Now . . . how many people would refuse to give their seat on a bus to a gray-haired lady on the basis that they were not required to follow God's law? How many would shove an old man out of the way to be first in line at the post office, on the same basis?

Or, to be even more blunt, how many people would argue against the verses in the same portion of the book of Leviticus that tell us not to have sexual relationships with our parents, our siblings, or our aunts and uncles?

This is God's *Torah,* given through the pen of Moses. It's also the same *Torah* that David loved, and which Paul proclaimed throughout his epistles, including the book of Romans.

5. Finally, to go beyond the sometimes humorous nature of some of the above and further clarify the point here, what law are modern believers in God truly NOT under? The answer to that question goes even farther beyond the scope of this study guide than all we've said up to this point, but perhaps the following points can help clarify the answer even if it can't be dealt with in detail in these pages.

Most of modern Christianity agrees that the Ten Command-ments and many of the accompanying Jewish *mitzvot* (guidelines for righteousness) still apply. But they specifically believe that modern Christians are not under any sacrificial, dietary, or seventh-day Sabbath laws.

THE "CURSE OF THE LAW"

Here's another concept that could be helpful to keep in mind when you read many of Paul's epistles, especially the segments that deal with the law.

Think of two parents who love their young daughter but also believe it is their duty to raise her to be respectful and responsible when she becomes a young woman. For that reason, they set boundaries and establish the "rules of the house" in which she grows up. These rules are all sound, established guidelines that cannot guarantee a perfect result because people are all different, but they all have one fundamental purpose.

The goal of those parents is to raise a daughter who is "righteous" in their eyes. That is, she honors their understanding of what it means to be a productive member of the family, culture, and larger society in which she will live, and in which she will represent them.

Now consider all this from the daughter's perspective. She dearly loves her parents, and in an ideal situation, she would do everything possible to live by their rules, even when she doesn't understand them or felt that they might be too confining.

Even so, as she grows up—and especially during her teenage years—no matter how conscientious or sincere the young girl is, chances are she will come into conflict with her parents at some point. Perhaps she will kick and scream when she is told to go to bed; maybe she will stay out too late and be grounded for a while. None of these experiences are pleasant for anyone involved, but they are normal parts of the growing-up process that even extend, many times, into adulthood. How many grown children have issues with their parents many years after they have left home?

On the other hand, consider what happens when a typical young girl—or a boy, for that matter—rebels against his or her parents. In many cases it's over in a few years, but in extreme cases it can lead to permanent problems between parent and child, in which almost everything the parent ever does will be resented, hated, and railed against. In such cases, the child often feels guilty about resisting even as he considers himself oppressed by the parents' rules, which are never quite fair.

Literally, that child has put himself "under the condemnation of the parents' law," with all the misery and disaffection that situation entails, through no fault whatsoever of the parents. And that brings us to the whole point of this discussion.

God is our Father. Very few of us go through our entire lives without

THE "CURSE OF THE LAW" (CONT.)

questioning Him at some point. Very few of us understand Him at every turn. And none of us, with the exception of His own Divine Son, have ever managed to observe every one of His guidelines for righteous living—even the simplest, most fundamental rules of conduct that we know He endorses.

But the point is, when we have a good relationship with Him we do not look upon His guidelines for righteous living as things that condemn us. We do not believe that His rules of conduct for us are too onerous, too heavy, or too difficult to live by, especially when we have His help available twenty-four hours a day.

(Note, also, that Moses said the same thing as above in Deuteronomy 30:11–14, as further explained—and compared to Paul's own words on the same subject—in the opening section of chapter 2 of this study guide.)

Instead, we look at them as guiding principles, as ways of measuring ourselves to know how we're doing. Think of David, writing in Psalm 1:2 and 40:8 of his absolute delight in the law of God! In similar ways, we can often be grateful too—for the chance to do something that pleases Him. And grateful also, almost inevitably, for the guidelines that help us understand what that something might be.

God Himself said that He had written the knowledge of His law upon our hearts (Jer. 31:33; Heb. 8:10). Perhaps that's why so many people, when they rebel against God, often feel lonely, depressed, and even vaguely guilty. This is perhaps the purest sense in which our failure to do what we know we should do brings about the "condemnation of the law" that many people speak of.

But our failures are not the fault of the guidelines, and they are not "fixed" by pretending that we have no obligations toward God except to do what feels good. Just as the rebellion of a child is "fixed" by acceptance and compliance with the laws and the guidelines that go with them, within that child's family and his society, so our disaffection from God is "fixed" by the very same thing.

Other modern Christians agree with the above, but they also believe in observing the dietary and seventh-day Sabbath laws that God Himself established.

No modern Christian groups with which the authors of this study guide are familiar would claim that they are still under the Old Testament sacrificial laws, for all seem to agree that these were abolished/replaced by Christ's death.

ONE FINAL POINT . . .

In another sense, Christ Himself answered the question of what "law" we are all under for the ancient Jews—and for us as well—when He spoke against some of what the earthly rabbis (and the Pharisees in particular), in the centuries leading up to His birth, had done to amplify, complicate, and add on, of their own interpretations and requirements, to God's original commands and guidelines. Paul reinforced the same basic concept in any number of places throughout the New Testament.

In other words, within Christianity we are not under any laws arising from man's add-ons to what God gave us, even if those add-ons have been around for centuries. Only God can create spiritual and moral laws (for example, "Do not commit adultery") and divine guidelines for how to keep them (for example, "Do not have sexual relations with your brother's wife").

Granted, man can create traditions and additional guidelines, but they are not equal to what came from the mouth of God. In spiritual matters, man's rules simply do not have the force of God's immutable laws.

The challenge, of course, is to remember which are which, and which should therefore have pre-eminence in our lives.

To a large extent, that is what the book of Romans is all about.

Beginnings

Romans 1:1–17

Before We Begin . . .

What do you believe was Paul's purpose in writing the book of Romans? What was he trying to accomplish?

Romans has been called one of the greatest doctrinal books in the Bible. Why do you think this might be so?

This short section of Romans includes a classic Pauline introduction to one of his letters, with one minor exception—he did not specifically name any of his intended recipients. Why this is true cannot be known with any degree of certainty, but many scholars believe it might have happened that way because Paul was not writing to any specific, single congregation—but instead, to "all who are in Rome, beloved of God, called to be saints" (Rom. 1:7 NKJV), exactly as he said.

Romans Chapter 1

From a Bondservant of Jesus Christ

Read the first seventeen verses of chapter 1, and then answer the following questions.

What is your conception of a "bondservant of Jesus Christ"? What did Paul mean by this expression?

What did Paul say he was called to be, in verse 1?

What did Paul say that God promised "through His prophets in the Holy Scriptures," in verse 2?

Paul said that Jesus Christ was "born of the seed of David according to the flesh," in verse 3. What does this mean?

In verse 4, Paul speaks of the "Spirit of holiness." Some commentators have suggested that this refers to Christ's own human *spirit, but most scholars agree that it means the Holy Spirit. What does Paul then refer to as the means by which we know that Christ is the Son of God? In other words, in addition to the witness of the Holy Spirit, what is the physical proof we also have?*

What are the two things that Paul then said we have received, in verse 5?

Why have we received these two things?

In verses 5 and 6, Paul makes it clear that he was called as an apostle to the Gentiles, "among all nations." In verse 6 he also explains that the individuals in the Roman congregation, as the recipients of his letter, were "also . . . the called of Jesus Christ," but not necessarily in the same way that he himself was. That is, Paul was called as an apostle; the members of the church at Rome were called by Christ to be believers in Him and to "be saints" on His behalf, as explained in verse 7.

This opening section then ends with the classic phrase, "Grace to you and peace from God our Father and the Lord Jesus Christ" (Rom. 1:7b NKJV).

PAUL'S DESIRE TO VISIT ROME

Next, Paul indicated that the faith of the members of the Roman congregation had already spread "throughout the whole world," which, in the reality of his day, probably included only the Roman Empire. This is a typical example showing how Paul established rapport with his readers, by including a testimony to their faith and a clear indication that he was faithful and diligent in praying for them.

In verse 9, how did he say that he made mention of them in his prayers—without what?

ABOUT THOSE EPISTLES . . .

Of the twenty-seven books in the New Testament, twenty-one are what we would call letters, or epistles, and almost two-thirds of those were written by Paul. Why is this particular literary form so well-represented in the New Testament?

The answer is not hard to come by, for in ancient times the epistolary form (that's another fancy word for letter) was just about the only game in town. Think about it. If Paul were in Jerusalem and wanted to communicate doctrinal advice to a group of believers in Rome, he could not pick up the phone and talk to a pastor. Neither could he send an e-mail, do a conference call, or even dash off a monologue and send a dozen copies. The fastest and most efficient way was to send a letter to a leader, who would then read it to the people.

Next, in verse 10, what did Paul say that he would like to do, if he could "find a way in the will of God"?

In verses 11–12, for what two reasons did he say that he longed to do so?

1.

2.

What additional reason did Paul give, in verse 13, for wishing to visit the church at Rome?

Who did he say that he was a debtor to, in verse 14? And, how did he then characterize each of the two groups he mentioned?

What did he say, in verse 15, that he was ready to do when he got to Rome?

THE JUST SHALL LIVE BY FAITH

The first half of chapter 1 ends with one of the most familiar of Paul's writings. This passage is shown below, with ten empty blank spaces replacing various words. Before you look them up, see how many you can fill in from memory, without referring to your Bible.

For I am not _____ of the _____ of Christ, for it is the _____ of God to _____ for everyone who believes, for the _____ first and also for the _____. For in it the _____ of God is revealed from faith to _____; as it is written, "The _____ shall live by _____." (Rom. 1:16–17 NKJV)

This particular passage also provides a brilliant illustration of something we have already mentioned back in the introduction to this study guide. In the ancient Hebrew language, Paul was known as a *gaon*, a "Torah genius," which essentially means that he had memorized the entire *tanakh* (Old Testament). Therefore he was able to quote from it at will as he often did while writing from prison without access to a written copy.

Here is the text from one of the less-familiar prophets, Habakkuk, from which Paul pulled the "quintessential quote" above:

> *I will stand my watch*
> *And set myself on the rampart,*
> *And watch to see what He will say to me,*
> *And what I will answer when I am corrected.*
> *Then the LORD answered me and said:*
> *"Write the vision*
> *And make it plain on tablets,*
> *That he may run who reads it.*
> *For the vision is yet for an appointed time;*
> *But at the end it will speak, and it will not lie.*
> *Though it tarries, wait for it;*
> *Because it will surely come,*
> *It will not tarry.*
> *"Behold the proud,*
> *His soul is not upright in him;*
> *But the just shall live by his faith.*
> *(Hab. 2:1–4 NKJV)*

THE SACRIFICE OF CHRIST GOES IN TWO DIRECTIONS

Here is another refinement on the understanding of blood sacrifices for sin in the Old Testament vs. Christ's sacrifice for sin in the New Testament. Many commentators believe that, even though God credited believers in ancient times with forgiveness of their sins through animal sacrifices, these sacrifices were not the true and complete mechanism by which God did so. Rather, they were forward-looking memorials to the ultimate sacrifice that would come later, that of God Himself through His Son Jesus Christ on the cross.

Thus Christ's sacrifice covered the sins of mankind for *all* time, not just from the Crucifixion forward. And, in a larger sense, the grace that God extended in Old Testament times becomes even more astounding to contemplate, because it was based on an event that had not happened yet according to the earthly measurement of time.

This is just one more example of the incomprehensible-to-man ways in which God Himself literally does His work outside of time—as only He can do.

PULLING IT ALL TOGETHER . . .

• Paul began the book of Romans with what would have been a classic introduction to a letter in that era. He identified himself, his recipients (although not by name), and then offered a brief salutation.

• Paul made it very clear that he was a dedicated servant of Jesus Christ, whose divinity as the Son of God is beyond question. Paul considered himself an apostle, sent to the Gentiles.

• Paul had not yet visited the church at Rome, but longed to do so.

• Paul ended this section with one of the most familiar of all Christian doctrinal statements: "The just shall live by faith." But this was not original with Paul—it can be found in the Old Testament, in Habakkuk 2:4.

Our Need for Righteousness

2

ROMANS 1:18–3:20

Before We Begin . . .

In this section of Romans, Paul makes it clear that he considers God's omnipotence, His omniscience, His majesty—indeed, His very existence itself—to be self-evident to all people via the obvious wonders of His creation. Do you agree with this assessment?

Based on everything we have written so far, and on your own understanding prior to reading this study guide, what is your understanding of the "need for righteousness" on our part? Why is this so important to God?

ROMANS CHAPTER 1:18–32

GOD'S WRATH ON UNRIGHTEOUSNESS

Paul began this section with a statement that harkens back to Moses' own words to the children of Israel, when he summarized all that God had given them just before he climbed his last mountain and was gathered to his fathers:

> "For this commandment which I command you today is not too mysterious for you, nor is it far off. It is not in heaven, that you should say, 'Who will ascend into heaven for us and bring it to us, that we may hear it and do it?' Nor is it beyond the sea, that you should say, 'Who will go over the sea for us and bring it to us, that we may hear it and do it?' But the word is very near you, in your mouth and in your heart, that you may do it." (Deut. 30:11–14 NKJV)

Compare what Moses said with what Paul wrote in the first four verses of this section:

For the wrath of God is revealed from heaven against all ungodliness and unrighteousness of men, who suppress the truth in unrighteousness, because what may be known of God is manifest in them, for God has shown it to them. For since the creation of the world His invisible attributes are clearly seen, being understood by the things that are made, even His eternal power and Godhead, so that they are without excuse, because, although they knew God, they did not glorify Him as God, nor were thankful, but became futile in their thoughts, and their foolish hearts were darkened. (Rom. 1:18–21 NKJV)

What did Moses say about what God expected of them—for example, was what He wanted too hard for them to understand?

Was it too "remote" or inaccessible to them?

What did Paul say about these very same things—was he in agreement with Moses, or not?

What did Paul specifically say about God's own attributes?

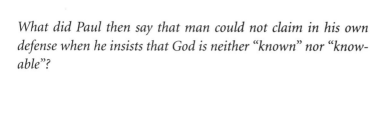

What did Paul then say that man could not claim in his own defense when he insists that God is neither "known" nor "knowable"?

What do you think is the basic message that both Moses and Paul were trying to get across?

Now read the remainder of chapter 1, starting with verse 22, and answer the questions below.

In verse 23, Paul spoke about "an image made like corruptible man." What was he really saying here—that is, what does humanity always seem to do, in almost all times and places, rather than simply worshiping the one true God?

What did Paul tell us that people "professing to be wise" often become, instead?

When that happens, what did Paul tell us that God then gives them up to, in verse 24?

What "exchange" did he tell us that such people have made?

What kind of passions did Paul speak about in verse 26?

In verse 27, how did Paul characterize the practices of men who burn "in their lust for one another"—that is, they are committing something that is . . . what?

To conclude this section, in verses 29–31, list all the things that Paul said both men and women who do what he spoke about previously would be filled with and/or would become.

Finally, do you believe Paul was right?

ROMANS CHAPTER 2

IS GOD'S JUDGMENT FAIR?

By what action did Paul say we often condemn ourselves, in verse 1?

In verse 2, did Paul say that the judgment of God works for or against those who "practice such things"?

What does the expression "such things" refer to?

In verse 3, Paul asked a question of "man"—but not just of any man. What words did Paul use to describe the man who will not escape the judgment of God?

In verse 4, Paul asked another question of "man," although he does not address him by name this time. What was Paul saying here about anyone who despises the "riches of His goodness, forbearance, and longsuffering"? Or, to put it another way, what did Paul say that such a person does not understand?

In verse 5, what are the two things that Paul said the same person is "treasuring up" for himself? Fill in the blanks below for the complete answers:

_____ *in the day of wrath and* _____ *of the righteous* _____ *of God . . . (from Rom. 2:5 NKJV)*

What did he say that God will do in response, in verse 6?

Following the above, what did Paul say that God will render, and to whom, in verses 7–10?

Fill in the blank in this well-known quote, from verse 11:

For there is no _____ *with God.*
(Rom. 2:11 NKJV)

Verses 12–16 can be understood to support some of what was included in the introduction to this study guide. Verse 13, for example, gives us the familiar "not hearers but doers" concept whereby Paul says it is not enough only to hear what is right, but that we must *do* what is right as well.

Then, in verse 14, Paul makes it clear that "Gentiles, who do not have the law" can still "by nature do the things in the law." In other words, even though a Gentile might not have been specifically taught to show respect to an older person as a matter of law (to reference the earlier example), such basic concepts are still written in their hearts and are the proper, righteous things to do for Gentiles as well as for Jews.

WHICH TESTAMENT CONTAINS THE MOST LAWS?

Virtually all of the 170 guidelines for righteousness of the Old Testament (see "Salvation Then and Now" in the introduction to this study guide), relating to what we might call "Christian conduct," are repeated in the New Testament via direct quotations (or paraphrases) of the Old. On the other hand, what is not so commonly realized is that, if you take every expression in which God says "do this" or "don't do that" in the New Testament, as expressed by Christ Himself, Paul, or the other canonical writers (who were writing under the inspiration of the Holy Spirit), the number of such laws in the New Testament is about 1,050.

Examples would include commands such as:
"Fear not" (Matt. 10:28, 31; Luke 8:50; Luke 12:32)
"Do not worry" (Matt. 6:31, 34; Matt. 10:19)
"Be joyful in hope, patient in affliction, faithful in prayer" (Rom. 12:12)
"In everything give thanks" (Eph. 5:20)
"Rejoice in the Lord always" (Phil. 4:4)
"Do nothing out of selfish ambition or vain conceit, but in humility consider others better than yourselves" (Phil. 2:3)

Surely all of the above should be taken as seriously and stringently as the law in Leviticus 19:32 about rising in honor of the gray-haired, and thus honoring the presence of an old person. Remember that the next time someone says that the Old Testament is a book of laws and the New Testament is a book of no laws, but only grace!

JEWS ARE AS GUILTY AS GENTILES

Fill in the blanks in the passage below, to see what Paul says to those who claim to be righteous "in the law" but do not necessarily do what they know they *should* do.

> *Indeed you are called a* _____, *and rest on the*
> _____, *and make your boast in God, and know*

*His will, and approve the things that are _____,
being instructed out of the law, and are _____
that you yourself are a guide to the blind, a light to those
who are in _____, an instructor of the foolish, a
teacher of babes, having the form of _____ and
truth in the law. You, therefore, who teach another, do
you not teach yourself? You who _____ that a
man should not steal, do you _____? You who
say, "Do not commit adultery," do you commit adultery? You who _____ idols, do you rob temples?
You who make your boast in the law, do you dishonor
God through breaking the law? For "the name of God is
_____ among the Gentiles because of you," as it
is written. (Rom. 2:17–24 NKJV)*

CIRCUMCISION OF NO AVAIL

In verses 25–29, Paul presented another of his better-known arguments in favor of what's in our hearts and not what we claim with our lips as the deciding factors in terms of what makes us true followers of Christ. The "circumcision of the heart" concept has been extracted many times, and used in many ways, to illustrate his point. Please read these verses carefully and answer the questions below.

Under what condition did Paul say that circumcision is indeed profitable, in verse 25?

What do you believe he meant by this?

What is the contrasting scenario he set up in verse 26?

How can verse 26 be reconciled (i.e., how does it agree or dis-agree) with what Paul said in verse 25?

SIN BY ANY DEFINITION . . .

Over the years, various scholars and teachers have provided any number of definitions of *sin,* ranging from the most horrific, high-profile sins against society (kidnapping, murder, etc.) to the least noticeable, near-hidden sins that occur only in private. In Romans 3:10–26, Paul provides an extended dissertation on the reality of sin within the hearts, minds, and actions of all men and women ever born, since Adam and Eve. As Paul says, " . . . all have sinned and fall short of the glory of God" (Rom. 3:23).

English translations of the New Testament may use any number of words to define sin in its various forms, but most are based on the following concepts—which, in turn, derive from certain Greek words in the original Greek text. Here are the six concepts, and their Greek roots, that occur most often in the New Testament. They are listed in order of most-frequently occurring to least-frequent.

Coming Short *(Gr: hamartia)*—failing, or missing the mark. Occurs more than 250 times in the New Testament.

Unrighteous; Iniquity *(Gr: adikia)*—doing wrong; being unjust; hurting others.

Trespass *(Gr: parapt?ma)*—falling, when you should have resisted or maintained your walk with the Lord.

Iniquity *(Gr: anomia)*—acting in a lawless manner.

Transgression *(Gr: parabasis)*—violating a specific law.

Ungodliness *(Gr: asebeia)*—living in rebellion against God and His standards.

What is the meaning of verses 28–29? What was Paul saying here? Can you put it in simpler terms, without losing any of his intended meaning?

ROMANS CHAPTER 3

JUSTIFICATION BY FAITH, NOT BY LAW

When Paul asked "What is the profit of circumcision?" (v. 1), clearly he was not talking about anything physical. What do you think he meant? What did he say, in the next three verses, that helps explain verse 1?

How can our unrighteousness demonstrate the righteousness of God, as Paul said in verse 5?

What was Paul's attitude toward God's right to judge humanity, in verse 6?

In verses 7–8, Paul made a point that can be vastly simplified by a common expression most of us have heard at one time or another. In truth it might also be somewhat of an oversimplification, but read these verses and see if you can fill in the blanks below with that ultra-familiar expression.

"Two _____ do not make a _____."

Do you think this simple expression applies to what Paul was saying in these verses? Why, or why not?

ALL HAVE SINNED

The next several verses—many of them quite familiar to students of the Bible—demonstrate once again Paul's mastery of the Scriptures. He quoted verses from several psalms, the book of Isaiah, and at least three of his own epistles, including the book of Romans.

Here is the most familiar portion of these verses. Fill in the blanks in this passage to see what Paul has to say about his contention that everyone ever born—with the exception of Jesus Christ Himself—was literally born into sin.

As it is written:
"There is none _____, no, not one;
There is none who understands;
There is none who _____ after God.
They have all turned aside;
They have together become _____;
There is none who does _____, no, not one.
Their throat is an open _____;
With their _____ they have practiced deceit;
The poison of asps is under their lips;
Whose mouth is full of _____ and bitterness.
Their feet are _____ to shed blood;
Destruction and misery are in their ways;
And the way of _____ they have not known.
There is no _____ of God before their eyes."
(Rom. 3:10–18 NKJV)

In verse 20, Paul once again reminded us of one of the major functions of *Torah* (i.e., the law), meaning both the Ten Commandments and the accompanying guidelines for righteousness that God provided in the Old Testament.

What is that function of those commandments and guidelines, as given to us by God to help us remain righteous in His sight—and also to help us minimize our sins, even though those sins are covered by the sacrifice of Christ?

PULLING IT ALL TOGETHER . . .

• Paul made it plain that the existence and the attributes of God should all be self-evident, through simple observance of His creation.

• Next, he told us that both God's judgments and, indeed, His very right to judge, are all eminently fair. Who else but the Creator of all things could possibly be qualified to judge His creation?

• Paul also told us that the Jews were just as guilty as the Gentiles, with respect to sinning against God. In that sense, circumcision is not a free ticket to righteousness—by itself it doesn't help.

• All of us, whether Jew or Gentile, are justified before God (i.e., He imputes righteousness to us so that He can look upon us as worthy to stand before Him) by putting our faith in Him, and not by simply following His Laws.

• None of us, in fact, is able to follow His Law so well that God could impute righteousness to us on that basis alone, for *all have sinned.*

How God Imputes Righteousness to Us

3

Romans 3:21–5:21

Before We Begin ...

If you have heard the expression "all have sinned," which appears in Romans 3:23, what is your understanding of its meaning? Do you believe it is a true statement?

When you think of Abraham, do you think of him as a Jew or a Gentile? Why?

Romans, Chapter 3:21–31

God's Righteousness through Faith

Paul began this section by reminding us that no one can earn their salvation (i.e., righteousness) through works, even if those works are based on rigid adherence to Scriptural principles as expressed in the Bible. At the same time, God's own infinite righteousness has already been established. As a result, our own righteousness, as imputed to us by God, can only come by faith in Him—which is the same as faith in Jesus Christ, for they are one and the same God. It can only be maintained by the ongoing forgiveness of our sin through the grace He extends to us by virtue of Christ's sacrifice on the Cross.

These basic principles have been given many different-sounding expressions throughout the history of Christianity, but essentially they all rest on the same fundamental truths, which Paul repeatedly reinforced. Read the remainder of chapter 21, and answer the following questions.

In verse 21, what did Paul say about how the righteousness of God is revealed?

Whom did he say, in verse 23, have fallen short of God's glory?

What do you believe Paul meant by "His forbearance" in verse 25?

Who is both "just and the justifier of the one who has faith in Jesus" in verse 26?

Verses 27–31 contain a number of important principles, some that might seem new and others that are clear reinforcements of previously established truths. To clarify this passage, let us break these five verses down into a series of simple statements, with additional explanations added as needed to further illuminate what Paul was saying.

VERSES 27–28

1. We have no right whatsoever to boast of our salvation. We did nothing to earn it—indeed, we *can't* earn it, no matter how hard we might try.

2. On the contrary, salvation is freely given to us by God, according to what Paul calls "the law of faith." This law must not be confused with anything else—Paul is simply saying that God always honors what He has long-since established as His fundamental, eternal, unchanging equation:

Faith and Trust in God = Salvation

3. This same salvation via faith in God was offered to the ancient Hebrews (God imputed righteousness to Abraham, Moses, David, and many others; see Romans 4:3) exactly as it was offered to the Jews and Gentiles of Paul's era, even as it is also offered to us here in the modern age.

VERSES 29–31

1. There is only one God—the same God who created the universe and all that's in it.

2. This same one God is the God of both the Jews and the Gentiles—the circumcised (Jews) and the uncircumcised (Gentiles).

3. All people from either one of these groups (which includes *everyone,* because you're either a Jew or you're not a Jew!) can be saved only through faith.

4. At the same time, because we cannot be eternally saved by observing what Judaism calls *Torah* and Christianity calls *the law,* that doesn't make the words that God gave to all humanity in the first five books of the Bible null and void.

5. On the contrary, all of this establishes the validity of those first five books, because we need God's guidance—and we need to follow His guidelines to the best of our ability—to live lives that please Him. That is, yes, our continuing sins are forgiven by virtue of Christ's sacrifice on the Cross, but we do not thereby have unlimited license to commit all kinds of sins on purpose, just to test and/or to take unlimited advantage of the continuing forgiveness He extends to us through His grace. God expects us to pursue a lifestyle that glorifies and honors Him, a lifestyle that demonstrates our allegiance to Him, a lifestyle that makes it obvious to others around us that we have faith in Him and therefore adhere to His teachings, to the extent that we are able.

6. In other words, our righteousness before God is the invisible, heavenly result of our faith and our trust in God, while our observance of His guidelines (i.e., our eagerness to conform to His image) is the visible, earthly result of that same faith and trust.

Indeed, the image of many new Christians comes to mind here—of people who are literally running after God, saying "What's my job? How can I help? What can I do to please You?" But again, it's not the "doing" that saves them; their zeal to serve Him is the result of their salvation—and of their gratitude for it—exactly as the same kind of zeal yielded the same attitude from Paul.

Many Christians believe, in fact, that it was that same radical, passionate nature of Paul's personality that made him so valuable to God. God saved Paul through a profound miracle of conversion on the Damascus Road, to get Paul on His own side and make him such a powerful, God-sent emissary to the rest of the world! As at least one teacher has said, Paul was "Peter on steroids," with the prior addition of extensive rabbinical training that enabled Paul to write down what God showed him in detailed yet coherent terms.

ROMANS CHAPTER 4

ABRAHAM WAS JUSTIFIED BY FAITH

The fourth chapter of Romans provides further commentary on what Paul said in the closing verses of chapter 3. It also expands on some of what we have already tried to extract and summarize in the previously-numbered points. Therefore, as a means of reinforcing and amplifying Paul's previous words (and also as a means of verifying our summary of them) please read chapter 4 of Romans and answer the following questions.

In verse 3, what did Paul say was the reason for which God "accounted" (or imputed) righteousness to Abraham?

In what verse did Paul say something very similar to Christ's own statement in Matthew 10:10: "for a worker is worthy of his food"?

DAVID CELEBRATES THE SAME TRUTH

What did Paul say about David, with respect to why righteousness was imputed by God to him? That is, was David considered righteous through his works?

ABRAHAM JUSTIFIED BEFORE CIRCUMCISION

What is the important distinction that Paul made, in verses 9 and 10, with respect to Abraham's faith being accounted for righteousness, by God?

What huge body of people did Paul refer to in these verses when he mentioned the "uncircumcised"?

What is the huge promise that Paul said that God extends to uncircumcised people (see question above) in verse 11, through the example of Abraham?

In what sense, then, is Abraham somewhat of a "crossover" example? And why is this aspect of Abraham's example so important to our understanding of the Bible today?

THE PROMISE GRANTED THROUGH FAITH

In verse 13, what did Paul say that Abraham's righteousness came through?

What did Paul say that Abraham's righteousness did NOT come through?

In verse 14, what did Paul say would be "made void" if we were able to attain righteousness by following the law?

What did "it is of faith that it might be according to grace" mean, in the first part of verse 16? (Hint: Read the remainder of verse 16 to get help with the answer!)

Verses 16b–22, in some places, are somewhat difficult to follow. Once again, let us see if we can extract the main points, one at a time:

1. Abraham (who was the genetic or "natural" father of the Jews and the spiritual father of all who came after him and believed in God), stood in the presence of God, in whom he (Abraham) believed.

2. God imputed Abraham's belief in Himself (God) as righteousness.

3. God promised Abraham that he would become the father of many nations, which is exactly what happened.

4. Meanwhile, because of the strength of his faith, Abraham was able to believe and trust in God when God told him that he would have a son, and thus many descendants through whom God's promises would be fulfilled, even though Abraham was close to one hundred years old when the promise of a son was given.

Paul closed chapter 4 with these words:

Now it was not written for his sake alone that it was imputed to him, but also for us. It shall be imputed to us who believe in Him who raised up Jesus our Lord from the dead, who was delivered up because of our offenses, and was raised because of our justification. (Rom. 4:23–25 NKJV)

Can you rephrase these verses, as you understand them? Try it in the space below.

WHEN WAS THE ANCIENT, PRIOR-TO-CHRIST SACRIFICIAL SYSTEM ESTABLISHED?

In the portion of Romans covered in this study guide chapter, Paul specifically talked about the reality of Abraham and David's salvation (i.e., the imputing of righteousness to them, by God), brought about through their faith in God. Some readers might experience minor difficulties in understanding this, for some have been taught that only those who accept salvation from God through the person of Jesus Christ can be saved.

This teaching ignores many things that happened prior to Christ's birth, but it's not the only familiar teaching that doesn't take Old Testament realities fully into account. For example, many who study the Bible believe that God established the sacrificial system, whereby men could sacrifice certain animals to atone for their sins (thus continually maintaining their righteousness before God), when He spoke to Moses on Mt. Sinai. This happened while the Israelites were on their way out of bondage in Egypt to the Promised Land of Canaan.

However, this "codifying action" actually came somewhat late in the history of God's relationship with His people. Many years before that, Noah sacrificed clean animals to God when he emerged from the ark (Gen. 8:20). He also knew the difference between clean and unclean animals when he loaded up the ark. Likewise, many years after the time of Noah (but long before Moses and Mt. Sinai), God Himself sacrificed a heifer in the process of establishing His eternal covenant with Abraham (Gen. 15:9–21).

Thus, what seems most likely is that many of the things God put in writing, through Moses, were already well-established between Himself and the ancient patriarchs, such as Noah and Abraham. Indeed, many of the rules of ancient covenant were not written down explicitly in the Bible, which explains why many who diligently study the Bible still have difficulty, sometimes, in understanding the basic nature and the sacred obligations of ancient Hebraic covenant—both those that were established between God and man (e.g., God and Noah/Abraham/Jacob) and those that were established between man and man (e.g., David and Jonathan).

In any case, clearly, it was partially by virtue of these common, ancient concepts that patriarchs such as Noah and Abraham could understand how to serve God so faithfully, long before all the rules of conduct were laid out officially.

ROMANS CHAPTER 5

FAITH TRIUMPHS IN TROUBLE

In chapter 5, Paul moved from the "how" to the "what" aspect of justification (or salvation) by faith in God. What did he say, in verses 1–4, that we both have and do as a result of that justification?

1. Things we have:

2. Things we do:

What did Paul say "produces perseverance" in verse 3?

What comes next? In other words, what is the complete three-unit sequence of things that are each produced, one after the other, by what Paul said (in v. 3) is the catalyst that starts the whole process?

In verse 5, what did Paul say "does not disappoint"?

And why did he say that is true?

In other words, what is the true and legitimate fulfillment of our hope, as detailed in these verses?

CHRIST IN OUR PLACE

Who did Paul say Christ died for, in verse 6?

In your own words, what do you see as the comparison Paul set up in verses 7–8, between Christ's willingness to die for our sin and the willingness of a typical person, in various situations, to do the same thing?

In verse 8, what did Christ demonstrate by His willingness to die for us while we were still sinners—and thus long before we could feel any gratitude toward Him?

Is Christ's willingness something that you, personally, can identify with? Do you believe that any other person on Earth would have the same willingness, in the same situation?

What did Paul say we are saved from, in verse 9, because we have been justified by His blood?

In verses 9–10, Paul twice used a classic "if this, then what about that?" semantic construct, which is common to ancient Hebrew writing. Here, the classic pattern goes like this:

If . . . we are "justified by His blood," *how much more shall we "be saved* from His wrath" (v. 9).

"If when we were enemies we were reconciled to God through the death of His Son, how much more shall we "be saved by His life" (v. 10).

Paul then extended these illustrations by one more level, in verse 11:

And not only that, but we also rejoice in God through our Lord Jesus Christ, through whom we have now received the reconciliation. (NKJV)

ANCIENT RULES OF BIBLICAL INTERPRETATION— LIGHT AND HEAVY

As was mentioned earlier in this study guide, Paul was a student of Gamaliel, who in turn was the grandson of Hillel and the one who continued Hillel's famous School of Hillel during Paul's lifetime. Hillel was famous for teaching the *Spirit of the Law* rather than the *Letter of the Law,* as Christ Himself also did.

As we also said earlier, Hillel was the first to write down the seven ancient rules of Scriptural interpretation, from the ancient Hebrew viewpoint, that are still in wide usage today. Indeed, many scholars believe that these rules were exactly what Paul meant when he mentioned "rightly dividing the Word of Truth" in 2 Timothy 2:15. These are the Hebraic rules of *biblical exegesis* (i.e., an explanation or an interpretation of something from the Bible) that were also observed in the writing of much of both the Old and New Testaments. For, on the other side of the equation (i.e., that of the writer), these also correspond to rules of logic and orderly presentation that Christ Himself often followed in His parables and other teachings.

A good example, in fact, of the training Christ Himself received as a young boy in the temple would be this principle, written down first by Hillel:

"What is hateful to you, do not do to your neighbor. . . that is the whole *Torah . . .*" which was later expressed by Christ as: "Therefore, whatever you want men to do to you, do also to them, for this is the Law and the Prophets" (Matt. 7:12 NKJV).

In the book of Romans we have many outstanding illustrations, written by Paul, of the first of those seven rules. This rule, called *Kal vahomer* ("light and heavy") in Hebrew, says that whatever truth applies in a less important case will apply in a more important case as well. Thus the phrase "how much more" (or something very similar) is often a signal that such an example is coming up. Two good illustrations of this from the Old Testament would include:

If the righteous will be recompensed on the earth,
How much more the ungodly and the sinner. (Prov. 11:31 NKJV)

If you have run with the footmen, and they have wearied you,
Then how can you contend with horses? (Jer. 12:5 NKJV)

From the New Testament, and directly from the mouth of Christ Himself, two excellent examples would include:

If a man receives circumcision on the Sabbath, so that the law of Moses
should not be broken, are you angry with Me because I made a man
completely well on the Sabbath?" (John 7:23 NKJV)

Then He said to them, "What man is there among you who has one sheep, and if it falls into a pit on the Sabbath, will not lay hold of it and lift it out? Of how much more value then is a man than a sheep? Therefore it is lawful to do good on the Sabbath." (Matt. 12:11–12 NKJV)

Many other examples of this kind of semantic construct can be found throughout the Bible, including—naturally—the letters of Paul! Consider these four examples from the 5th chapter of Romans alone. Italics have been added to emphasize how closely Paul followed the classic light/heavy concept.

Much more then, having now been justified by His blood, we shall be saved from wrath through Him. (Rom. 5:9 NKJV)

For if when we were enemies we were reconciled to God through the death of His Son, much more, having been reconciled, we shall be saved by His life. (Rom. 5:10 NKJV)

For if by the one man's offense many died, much more the grace of God and the gift by the grace of the one Man, Jesus Christ, abounded to many. (Rom. 5:15 NKJV)

For if by the one man's offense death reigned through the one, much more those who receive abundance of grace and of the gift of righteousness will reign in life through the One, Jesus Christ. (Rom. 5:17 NKJV)

DEATH IN ADAM, LIFE IN CHRIST

In verse 12, how did Paul say that sin entered the world?

How did he say that death entered the world?

50

How did he then say that death thus spread throughout the world?

In verse 13, when did Paul say that sin was not imputed? Why would this be true?

Who, in verse 14, did Paul say Adam was a "type" of?

In verse 16, what did Paul say that the "free gift which came from many offenses" resulted in?

Paul concluded the chapter with five well-known verses. Fill in the blanks in the spaces below to see what those verses say.

Therefore, as through one man's _____ judgment came to all men, resulting in _____, even so through one Man's righteous act the free gift came to all men, resulting in _____ of life. For as by one man's disobedience many were made sinners, so also by one Man's _____ many will be made righteous. Moreover the law entered that the

_____ might abound. But where sin abounded,
_____ abounded much more, so that as sin
reigned in death, even so grace might reign through
_____ to eternal life through Jesus Christ our
Lord. (Rom. 5:18–21 NKJV)

PULLING IT ALL TOGETHER . . .

• Abraham was justified (i.e., made righteous, or "saved") by his faith in God.

• The same was true for David—and by extension for other Old Testament patriarchs as well, who were all followers of God through their faith and not by their works.

• Abraham, in fact, was justified by faith before he was circumcised, meaning that circumcision is no more than a sign of the covenant with God, and not the basis of salvation. And this, of course, is true of any other work.

• The same faith that was accounted as righteousness in Abraham should be a tremendous source of strength, to believers, in times of trouble. (Indeed, it certainly carried Abraham through times of severe testing!)

• Christ died in our place, for our sin.

• Thus, though humanity received a sentence of death via the sin of Adam, we receive life through the sacrifice of Christ.

How We Achieve Righteousness

4

ROMANS 6:1–8:39

Before We Begin ...

Do you already have a favorite verse from Romans? If so, write it here.

If you have read Romans before, what do you believe was Paul's ultimate reason for writing it?

ROMANS CHAPTER 6

DEAD TO SIN, ALIVE TO GOD

The opening verses of this chapter contain another of Paul's best-remembered statements:

> *What shall we say then? Shall we continue in sin that grace may abound? Certainly not!* (Rom. 6:1–2a NKJV)

This opening statement is a logical follow-up to what Paul wrote in chapter 5, in which he explained that God's grace, via the death of Christ, covers our sin once we believe in Him and accept His free gift. But we cannot properly "build the volume of grace" in our lives by expanding the volume of sin, any more than a naughty child can properly misbehave to earn more forgiveness from his parents—and more hugs and kisses once each round of discipline is over!

Read the first twelve verses of this chapter and answer the questions below.

What did Paul say, in verse 3, with respect to being "baptized into Christ Jesus"? What were we also baptized into?

By being baptized into His death, and then being "buried with Him through baptism into death" (which is essentially the whole salvation process), what is it that we also became "dead" to through that process?

If you said "sin" above, you are right! But in verse 4, Paul then tells us what should be the result of that "death." In his own words, what was that result?

In your own words, what did he mean by saying that we "should walk in newness of life"?

In verse 6 we find another well-known reference by Paul, to the "old man." Who is this "old man" he is talking about, who was "crucified with Him"?

What, therefore (v. 6), was "done away with" by our crucifixion "with Him"?

Finally, after building his case in step-by-step, logical fashion, Paul brought it all together in the following passage. Please fill in the blanks, below, to make this passage your own!

> *For he who has died has been _____ from sin. Now if we died with Christ, we believe that we shall also _____ with Him, knowing that Christ, having been _____ from the dead, dies no more. Death no longer has _____ over Him. For the death that He died, He died to sin once for all; but the life that He lives, He lives to God. Likewise you also, reckon your- selves to be dead indeed to sin, but _____ to God in Christ Jesus our Lord. (Rom. 6:7–11 NKJV)*

In verse 12, what did Paul then say about letting sin "reign in your mortal body"?

55

What did he say, in verse 13, that we should not do?

Finally, Paul ended this section with the following passage:

> *For sin shall not have dominion over you, for you are not under law but under grace. (Rom. 6:14 NKJV)*

This particular verse can be interpreted several different ways. Taken completely out of context—and forgetting entirely that Paul was a Jewish rabbi speaking to a group of Romans of whom many were, themselves, devout followers of biblical Judaism—it is possible to construe this verse to mean that believers in Christ are not under any law whatsoever. In other words, by logical extension, if we say that we are absolutely not under any law, we would be interpreting Paul as saying that we need not obey any of the commandments God gave us in the Old Testament. (And these commandments, of course, include things as serious as murder and as relatively benign as not standing up when an older person enters the room.)

However, most Christians agree that Paul used the word "under" with reference to the *condemnation* of the law, which comes ONLY to those who try to "make themselves righteous before God" by strict self-observance of the law rather than by trusting in God, by faith, for their salvation (righteousness).

Thus Paul's message here is actually quite simple. We cannot do it ourselves. If we try to be righteous before God via our own efforts, so that we can stand before Him as moral equals, we will always fail.

To put this in a larger context (and thus, perhaps, to help resolve the occasional confusion between Old Testament and New Testament salvation mechanisms), even as the ancient believers in the Old Testament had to have their sin covered (i.e., forgiven) via blood sacrifices, we in the post-Christ world must have our sin covered (i.e., forgiven) by accepting the grace that Christ offers through His own death on the cross.

In other words, this verse does not give anyone a license to do anything their carnal nature might like them to do! It is simply an admonition, from Paul, not to be so proud and arrogant that we would try to remain free-from-sin in our own strength and on our own volition.

It cannot be done.

FROM SLAVES OF SIN TO FREEDOM IN GOD

In the remainder of this chapter, Paul dealt with some of the questions and potential misunderstandings that he felt might arise, logically, out of what he had already said. He amplified his meaning and provided a number of vivid examples, to illustrate what he was saying.

In verse 15, did Paul say we have a license to sin as much as we want—yes or no?

In your own words, how would you summarize the message of verses 16–20? Paul was using the metaphor of slavery to explain his meaning—how do you interpret that metaphor?

To conclude this chapter and—once again!—to help bring Paul's words alive, fill in the blanks in the passage below.

> *For when you were slaves of sin, you were free in regard to _____. What fruit did you have then in the things of which you are now _____? For the end of those things is _____. But now having been set free from sin, and having become slaves of God, you have your fruit to holiness, and the end, _____*
>
> *_____. For the wages of sin is death, but the gift of God is _____ _____ in Christ Jesus our Lord. (Rom. 6:20–23 NKJV, emphasis added)*

esu NOT UNDER THE LAW . . .

We have already examined Romans 6:14 ("we are not under law, but under grace") at length, but two additional points could be made.

First, by his usage of the word translated as "law," Paul could have been referring to what we often consider excessive "legalism," which in this case might be defined as the tendency to overlay God's Word with manmade additions and refinements (as the ancient Pharisees sometimes did, for which Christ scolded them quite vehemently). Clearly, we are not required to follow man's traditions ahead of God's commandments. At the same time, John 10:22–23 tells us that Christ went to the temple in Jerusalem to observe the *Feast of Dedication,* which is now called *Hanukah.* This tells us that it's perfectly all right to honor the traditions of men as long as they do not conflict with, or take precedence over, what God tells us to do in His own Word.

Second, Paul could have been implying that, even as we formally put ourselves under God's grace, through baptism, we are given additional strength to "die to sin" and thus be less susceptible to its temptations.

ROMANS CHAPTER 7

THE LAW CANNOT SAVE US FROM SIN

In the beginning of this chapter, Paul used another vivid metaphor, that of a woman whose husband dies. While he lived, they were bound together by the laws of marriage, and thus they had legal obligations, both moral and civil, to each other. But when he died, those obligations died with him—although common custom would suggest that the woman might want to honor her husband's memory. Nonetheless, the woman's second marriage, which would have been illegal while her first husband was alive, would be completely legal and honorable after her first husband passed away.

Paul then extended the metaphor by contrasting those people who would try to achieve righteousness via the law, through their own efforts, with those who "die" to that false notion, become "married" to Christ, and thus achieve righteousness through His grace.

Verse 6 seems especially meaningful: "But now we have been delivered from the law, having died to what we were held by, so that we should serve in the newness of the Spirit and not in the oldness of the letter" (Rom. 7:6 NKJV).

Clearly, what Paul meant by "what we were held by" would be the very concept of salvation via observance of the law. Given that, what do you think Paul meant by "newness of the Spirit" versus "oldness of the letter"? Would it be, essentially, the same thing?

Given what you already know about Christ's own stance on spiritual matters, would He have been more inclined toward the "spirit" or the "letter" of the law, as Paul defined them? Likewise, can you think of any examples in which Christ demonstrated His take on this subject?

In verse 7, did Paul tell us that the law, per se, is sin?

What did he identify, in the same verse, as the proper function of the law?

In verse 8, what did Paul say that sin was able to do, by "taking opportunity by the commandment"?

Let us trace the logic of what Paul was saying, in verses 8–12:

1. The law identified sin as sin. But the carnal, defiant nature of humankind is such that it naturally lusts after sin and desires to do it (v. 8). Thus Paul said that knowing what sin was produced the desire to pursue it.

2. Paul then said (v. 9) that, although he was "alive" (meaning that he was probably what we might call a "decent guy"), when he did not know or observe God's laws, once he awoke to the significance of the law (for example, "Do not covet"), he died in a spiritual sense under the judgment of the law he had broken.

3. In an overall sense, sin is like a personal enemy that resides within us. Paul therefore said, in verse 12, that the law, by contrast, is holy, just, and good, because it identifies what we should be and what we should do.

Paul then went on to add additional clarification of the above. For example, what did he say was producing death in him, in verse 13? (Hint: Think of the law as a spotlight, shining on certain things . . .)

What did Paul say that the nature of the law is, versus the nature of sin, in verse 14?

Why would this distinction matter? What do you believe Paul was trying to convey by emphasizing this distinction?

What do you believe is the overall message of verses 15–20? Try to "sketch it out," as we have done with previous sections, in the space provided. These are numbered for your convenience, but you can certainly add or subtract numbers as necessary.

1.

2.

3.

4.

5.

6.

Finally, in verses 21–25, Paul gave us a brilliant summary of the dilemma in which he found himself outside of an ongoing relationship with God, starting with salvation. That is, he found himself wanting to do right but inclined by nature to do evil; he literally found his body warring against what his mind told him was right.

Once again, let us end this section with Paul's own words. Fill in the blanks.

> *I find then a law, that evil is _____ with me, the one who wills to do good. For I _____ in the law of God according to the inward man. But I see another law in my _____, warring against the law of my mind, and bringing me into _____ to the law of sin which is in my members. O wretched man that I am! Who will _____ me from this body of death? I thank God—through Jesus Christ our Lord! So then, with the mind I myself serve the law of God, but with the _____ the law of sin.* (Rom. 7:21–25, NKJV)

WHAT IS "LEGALISM"?

Historically, the term "legalism" has been thrown about in many different contexts, at different times. For example, in Paul's day certain Jews were known as "Judaizers," another name for legalists. This came about because they insisted that Gentiles who wanted to accept Christ as Messiah/Savior had to become full-fledged Jews first, with all the traditional trappings of the faith, not to mention the extensive training and the acceptance of an entire system of new rules and regulations that such a conversion could entail.

Likewise, in effect, Christ called the Pharisees legalists for their adherence to their own highly evolved, extremely complicated system of manmade laws that lay like a smothering blanket over the comparatively spare, simple commandments that God Himself had given them.

In more recent times, believers in Christ who do not agree with mainline Christianity in various doctrinal matters—such as when God's Sabbath should be observed—are often called legalists. In other words, the definition depends entirely on who's doing the defining and who's being defined. If person *A* believes Principle *A*, and person *B* believes Principle *A*+1, then *A* is a "legalist" from *B*'s point of view. Or, maybe *B* is a legalist from from *A*'s point of view!

ROMANS CHAPTER 8

FREE FROM INDWELLING SIN

In verse 1, what do those who walk with Christ, according to the Spirit, not have to worry about?

In verse 2, Paul said that the law of the Spirit of life in Christ Jesus had freed him from the law of . . . what?

What the law could not do because it depended on the flesh (i.e., on us), Paul told us in verse 3 that God did by doing what?

After God sent His own Son, what did He then condemn?

And why did He do that?

In verse 5, what did Paul say that those who live according to the flesh set their minds on?

What about those who live according to the Spirit?

To be carnally minded is equivalent to what, in verse 6?

Why is this so?

Can those who are "in the flesh" please God, according to verse 8?

How do we know whether we are "in the flesh" or "in the Spirit," according to verse 9?

If Christ is in us (v. 10), what is therefore "dead" and what is therefore "life"? Why?

In verse 11, what did Paul say will happen to our mortal bodies through His Spirit, who dwells in us?

SONSHIP THROUGH THE SPIRIT

What did Paul say is the key to life, in verse 13?

Must you do this alone?

Who, in verse 14, did Paul identify as the "sons of God"?

In a few of these verses—in particular, verses 15–17—Paul used the word "spirit" in a way that might be confusing to modern ears, especially since it is juxtaposed against the capitalized "Spirit of God." But do not be confused by this. As an example, when Paul referred in verse 15 to the "spirit of bondage" versus the "Spirit of adoption" (the latter capitalized because it refers to something coming directly from God), he simply meant to be referencing all those feelings, obligations, and benefits that go with bondage (to sin) and adoption (by God). In that context, then, it is clearly a far better thing to have the feelings, obligations, and benefits of adoption by God, as His sons and daughters, rather than those of bondage to sin.

From Suffering to Glory

What did Paul not consider worthy to be compared with the glory that will one day be revealed in each of us, through Christ?

Read the following verses (which we have broken apart into sentence-by-sentence order), then write a short explanation in the numbered spaces provided. Do it point-by-point, if possible—numbering should help you organize your thoughts. What was Paul saying here? What did he mean by "the creation"? Who are the "children of God"? And what, in the end, what did Paul tell us is the value of hope?

For the earnest expectation of the creation eagerly waits for the revealing of the sons of God.

For the creation was subjected to futility, not willingly, but because of Him who subjected it in hope; because the creation itself also will be delivered from the bondage of corruption into the glorious liberty of the children of God.

For we know that the whole creation groans and labors with birth pangs together until now.

Not only that, but we also who have the firstfruits of the Spirit, even we ourselves groan within ourselves, eagerly waiting for the adoption, the redemption of our body.

For we were saved in this hope, but hope that is seen is not hope; for why does one still hope for what he sees?

But if we hope for what we do not see, we eagerly wait for it with perseverance.
(Rom. 8:19–25 NKJV)

1.

2.

3.

4.

5.

6.

In verse 26, who did Paul say will help us in our weaknesses?

For whom does the Spirit make intercession? And whom do you believe Paul meant by the "saints" in verse 27?

Next, we come to one of the best-known verses in all of Christendom. Rather than try to answer questions or fill in blanks, let us just rejoice in its certainty, for it is true even if we do not always understand the how and the why of God's purposes for us!

> *And we know that all things work together for good to those who love God, to those who are the called according to His purpose. (Rom. 8:28 NKJV)*

Verses 29 and 30 cannot be fully discussed in a study guide as limited as this! Just as huge books have been written on the book of Romans (see "The Romans Irony" in chapter 5), thousands of words have also been written about these two verses. Therefore, please consider just one or two questions, then do some additional research and decide how you believe these particular verses should be interpreted.

In verse 29, when Paul spoke of those whom God "foreknew," did he mean, specific, individual people whom God selected Himself, or did he mean the entire group of believers, down through the centuries, who have accepted God's Son as their Messiah/Savior? God surely knew that this would happen, and because He operates outside of our dimension of time, He undoubtedly knew/knows which individuals would respond.

Does God's limitless knowledge of all things, in all times and places, mean that He makes all those things happen?

Likewise, in the same verse, when Paul told us that God therefore has prepared a heavenly home in which all of those people who accepted salvation through faith would be "brethren" with Christ, does that mean that God will make up the guest list Himself, or does He offer the right to come—truly—to anyone and everyone who would accept it?

The way you answer those questions will determine how you interpret Romans 8:29–30. And here is the main question again, in a simpler form:

God knows all things. So . . . does that mean He also causes all things?

GOD'S EVERLASTING LOVE

What is the well-known "evangelical statement" of hope and assurance contained within verse 31?

Why Was the Firstborn So Important?

In Romans 8:29, Paul spoke of Christ in these terms: "that He might be the firstborn among many brethren." In the ancient Hebrew culture, being firstborn meant being most important in a legal sense, and most honored in a family setting. Thus, most of us in the modern age are familiar with one of the rights of the firstborn son of a king, to be made the monarch when his father passed away.

In Hebrew society, the firstborn also had responsibilities and functions to go along with his rights. For example, the firstborn was expected to take the lead in caring for his parents when they grew old. Another classic example—but this time demonstrating the occasional clash between rights and responsibilities—involves one of the best-known Old Testament conflicts between two brothers, Jacob and Esau, who both wanted the paternal blessing of Isaac. The firstborn was Esau, to whom fell the duty of the firstborn in each family to tend the family campfire and keep the communal pot cooking. Thus Jacob (the younger) cooked lentil stew while Esau (the elder) went hunting. Even so, most readers note Jacob's duplicity but seem entirely unaware of Esau's failure to live up to one of his own responsibilities.

In any case, calling anyone the firstborn implied a position of honor and respect—as well as duty and responsibility—that no one else would be expected to shoulder as long as the firstborn lived. In the case of Jesus Christ, calling Him the "firstborn among many brethren" elevates us as well, for thus we are known as His rightful brothers and sisters.

Who did Paul tell us God did not spare, in verse 32?

What is the logical construction Paul set up in verse 32—if He did not spare His own Son, then . . . what?

Who makes intercession for us, at the right hand of God?

What are the seven things that Paul said should not separate us from the love of Christ, in verse 35?

One more time, let us end this study guide chapter with the final verses from another of Paul's chapters in Romans. And again, no blanks to fill in or questions to answer; on the contrary, this would be a terrific passage to memorize exactly as it appears below:

> *Yet in all these things we are more than conquerors through Him who loved us. For I am persuaded that neither death nor life, nor angels nor principalities nor powers, nor things present nor things to come, nor height nor depth, nor any other created thing, shall be able to separate us from the love of God which is in Christ Jesus our Lord. (Rom. 8:37–39 NKJV)*

PULLING IT ALL TOGETHER . . .

• Christ's sacrifice, through the grace of God, covers our sin but does not give us license to sin as much as we want.

• No one can make himself righteous before God via his own efforts to follow the law.

• In a metaphorical sense, we should be willing slaves to God rather than unwilling slaves to sin.

• Even though we do not always understand His purposes, God does work things out for us for our own good.

• Absolutely nothing can ever separate us from the love of God.

THE TRIUMPH OF RIGHTEOUSNESS

5

ROMANS 9:1–11:36

Before We Begin ...

Based on all that the book of Romans has made clear to this point, what do you believe will be Paul's take on how we can achieve righteousness? By Whom, and through what mechanism?

Taken together, chapters 9, 10, and 11 of the book of Romans have often been called one of the most important passages in the Bible. Not all Christians interpret all these verses in precisely the same way, but all would certainly agree that they deal with some of the most important questions we can ask, including the un-spoken question that Paul might have had in mind as he wrote. By extending sal-vation to the Gentiles, has God in any way broken or even compromised the divine promises He long before extended to the Jews, to make them—forever—His cho-sen people?

As with other aspects of Romans, it is beyond both the scope and the intent of this study guide to advocate any single answer to that question. Instead, let us focus on what Paul actually says so that each one who studies Romans may be led to a God-given understanding.

ROMANS CHAPTER 9

ISRAEL'S REJECTION OF CHRIST DOES NOT ALTER GOD'S PURPOSES

What did Paul tell us he had in his heart, in verse 2?

Paul's reason for the feelings listed is his realization that Israel had rejected her Messiah. In verses 3–5, he told us that he would rather bear a curse from God on behalf of his Israelite brethren, if by so doing he could cause them to believe.

In verses 6–7, what do you believe Paul meant when he said "for they are not all Israel who are of Israel, nor are they all children because they are the seed of Abraham"? (Hint: Try comparing the single word "Israel" with the two words "of Israel.")

Paul then clarified the above in verse 8, by essentially saying that those who are the "children of the flesh" are not the children of God, whether Jews or Gentiles. Conversely, those who truly are the "children of God," meaning those who believe in Him and accept salvation, can be either Jews or Gentiles yet are all of one family in Christ.

ISRAEL'S REJECTION AND GOD'S JUSTICE

In verse 14, did Paul allow the possibility of unrighteousness with God?

The following is another well-known passage. Fill in the blanks to see what Paul was saying about God and His mercy.

For He says to Moses, "I will have __Mercy__ on whomever I will have mercy, and I will have _____ on whomever I will have compassion." So then it is not of him who wills, nor of him who

_____, but of God who shows mercy. For the Scripture says to the _____, "For this very purpose I have raised you up, that I may show My _____ in you, and that My name may be declared in all the earth." Therefore He has mercy on whom He wills, and whom He wills He _____.
(Rom. 9:15–18 NKJV)

What did Paul mean, in verse 21, when he spoke of the potter and the clay? Who is the potter and who is the clay? What rights and obligations does each one have to the other?

Who are the "vessels of wrath" in verse 22? Who prepared them for destruction?

Who are the "vessels of mercy" in verses 23–24? Who prepared them for glory?

In verses 25–26, most commentators believe that Paul quoted Hosea 2:23 and Hosea 1:10 to show that God has extended His acknowledgement of the Jews, as His sons, to the Gentiles as well. He then quoted Isaiah 10:22, to the effect that only a minority of the children of Israel (a remnant) would be saved, although the nation itself might become very large. He also explained, in verse 29, that what had happened to Israel in the past could very well happen again in the future.

PRESENT CONDITION OF ISRAEL

In verse 30, Paul summarized what this chapter is all about via an emphatic restatement of classic Christian doctrine: That the Gentiles, "who did not pursue righteousness" have nonetheless been given the privilege of attaining righteousness through faith in God. Paul then contrasts this fact with an ironic reference to many of the Jews, who rejected faith in Christ in favor of vain attempts to achieve righteousness through their own works.

The message is very clear: Salvation is for all, but only through faith and not by works.

ROMANS CHAPTER 10

SALVATION IS OPEN TO ALL

In chapter 10, Paul segued from the past to the present. What did he say is the desire of his heart, in verse 1?

What is the indictment that Paul brought against the Jews, in verses 2–4? What had the Jews failed to do, and what had they done instead?

In verse 8, what did Paul say is "near you, in your mouth and in your heart"?

Fill in the blanks in the following passage, to see what Paul stated as fundamental Christian doctrine with respect to salvation.

> . . . *that if you* _____ *with your mouth the Lord Jesus and* _____ *in your heart that God has raised Him from the dead, you will be* _____. *For with the heart one believes unto* _____, *and with the mouth* _____ *is made unto salvation. For the Scripture says, "Whoever believes on Him will not be put to shame." For there is no* _____ *between Jew and Greek, for the same Lord over all is rich to all who call upon Him. For "whoever calls on the name of the* LORD *shall be* _____." *(Rom. 10:9–13 NKJV)*

ISRAEL REJECTS THE GOSPEL

What are the four anomalies (i.e., the logical inconsistencies) that Paul identified in verse 14? (Hint: The first one is listed below.)

1. You can't ask for help from someone you don't believe has any power to help you.

2.

3.

4.

IS CHRIST THE "END" OF THE LAW?

Romans 10:4, says: "For Christ is the end of the law for righteousness to everyone who believes." This particular verse has been understood for centuries to mean that Christ's death on the Cross brought about a total cessation of the need for believers in Him to observe any of the laws He gave us in the Old Testament. We dealt with the general thrust of this understanding in the introduction to this study guide by explaining that the word so often translated into English as "law" should be *Torah* for those who understand Hebrew, or something similar to "guidelines for righteous living" for those who read only English.

However, many scholars believe that the word "end" in this context has been misunderstood even more than the word "law," for it does not mean "termination" at all, but "goal." A good comparison might be drawn between this usage of the word "end" and its same usage in a book by a well-known social critic written in 1995, called *End of Education*. That book did not argue that education had "ended" in America; on the contrary, it asked a series of questions about what the goal of education in America ought to be.

Perhaps *Vines Expository Dictionary of Old and New Testament Words* says it best—that the Greek word *telos* in Romans 10:4, almost always translated as "end" in English, should be defined as "the final issue or result of a state or process." In other words, as Paul has already said more than once, the law (i.e., *Torah*) witnesses to the righteousness of God, and Christ Himself *is* the law in the flesh. That is, He is the goal or the *final result* toward which all of the so-called "law" points.

Why do you think Paul included the "beautiful feet" quotation, from Isaiah, in verse 15? What was he trying to illustrate?

Verse 16 contains Paul's classic explanation of where faith comes from. What did he say?

What do you believe is the general "thrust" of Paul's quotations from Isaiah, in verses 18–21? What do they say about the responsibility of the Jews relative to their own salvation?

ROMANS CHAPTER 11

JEWS AND GENTILES ARE GRAFTED INTO ONE TREE

What did Paul say, in verses 1–2, about whether God had abandoned His chosen people?

What example did Paul use in verses 3–4 to prove the above?

Fill in the blanks in the verse below.

> *And if by _____, then it is no longer of _____; otherwise grace is no longer grace. But if it is of _____, it is no longer _____; otherwise work is no longer work. (Rom. 11:6 NKJV)*

THE ROMANS IRONY

Virtually all of modern Christianity comes down on one side or the other of a series of teachings that originated (or, at the very least, were first cohesively expressed by) a 16th-century man named John Calvin. After his death, Calvin's teachings were turned into a system of theology that eventually came to be called "Calvinism." Calvinism puts forth five basic precepts that are made memorable by the acronym TULIP, which stands for (1) Total Depravity, (2) Unconditional Election, (3) Limited Atonement, (4) Irresistible Grace, and (5) Perseverance of the Saints.

Like so many other deeper issues that even the briefest excursion into the book of Romans brings up, a discussion of the pros and cons of Calvinism is simply way beyond the scope of this study guide. So what is our point?

Only that the book of Romans, ironically, is used by both sides in the debate over the theological viability of Calvinism, sometimes also called the *Doctrine of Election* (meaning that only the "elect" can be saved), versus its counterpart, the *Doctrine of Free Will,* which teaches that we all have free will to choose or reject salvation. The "election" side uses Romans 3:12, 8:28, and 8:29–30 to help prove its case. The "free will" side uses Romans 1:16, 3:10–18, and 8:28.

To decide for yourself, read any of the numerous books on the subject . . . and, read Romans carefully!

ISRAEL'S REJECTION IS NOT FINAL

In verse 11 Paul said that salvation had come to the Gentiles. What did he say that meant with respect to the Jews—to provoke the Jews to what?

How did Paul say that he magnified his ministry to the Jews (i.e., "those who are my flesh") in verses 13–15?

The following passage, taken from the 11th chapter of Romans, is one of Paul's best-known illustrations of the dynamic between Jews and Gentiles—that is, between the root and the branches, the domesticated olive tree and the wild olive tree.

Directly below this passage from Romans we have inserted another well-known passage, which is a direct quotation from Christ Himself, taken from the 15th chapter of the book of John. Please read each of these passages carefully, compare them to each other, and then answer the questions following the second passage.

Passage 1: Romans 11:17–24 NKJV

[17]*And if some of the branches were broken off, and you, being a wild olive tree, were grafted in among them, and with them became a partaker of the root and fatness of the olive tree,* [18]*do not boast against the branches. But if you do boast, remember that you do not support the root, but the root supports you.*

[19]*You will say then, "Branches were broken off that I might be grafted in."* [20]*Well said. Because of unbelief they were broken off, and you stand by faith. Do not be haughty, but fear.* [21]*For if God did not spare the natural branches, He may not spare you either.* [22]*Therefore consider the goodness and severity of God: on those who fell, severity; but toward you, goodness, if you continue in His goodness. Otherwise you also will be cut off.* [23]*And they also, if they do not continue in unbelief, will be grafted in, for God is able to graft them in again.* [24]*For if you were cut out of the olive tree which is wild by nature, and were grafted contrary to nature into a cultivated olive tree, how much more will these, who are natural branches, be grafted into their own olive tree?*

Passage 2: John 15:1–8 NKJV

*"I am the true vine, and My Father is the vinedresser.
²Every branch in Me that does not bear fruit He takes
away; and every branch that bears fruit He prunes, that
it may bear more fruit. 3You are already clean because
of the word which I have spoken to you. ⁴Abide in Me,
and I in you. As the branch cannot bear fruit of itself,
unless it abides in the vine, neither can you, unless you
abide in Me.*

*⁵"I am the vine, you are the branches. He who abides
in Me, and I in him, bears much fruit; for without Me
you can do nothing. ⁶If anyone does not abide in Me, he
is cast out as a branch and is withered; and they gather
them and throw them into the fire, and they are burned.
⁷If you abide in Me, and My words abide in you, you
will ask what you desire, and it shall be done for you.
⁸By this My Father is glorified, that you bear much fruit;
so you will be My disciples."*

*In what ways do these two passages complement and reinforce
each other?*

*In what ways do they use similar metaphors yet focus on
different aspects of the relationships between the Jews and the
Gentiles, and between all believers and God Himself?*

When Paul said that "all Israel will be saved," in verse 26, do you think he meant all of the Nation of Israel *or all of* believing Israel?

Verse 28 can be a bit difficult to understand. However, most commentators believe Paul was saying that the Jews were "enemies" of the gospel in the sense that—by their rejection of Christ—they made the gospel available to the Gentiles. The other half of the picture, however, is that the Jews will always be beloved of God for the "sake of the fathers," meaning Abraham, Isaac, and Jacob from whom the Jews all came. Verses 29–32 then elaborate on these basic points.

Chapter 11 ends with this profound statement—again, one that is so very familiar to Christians all over the world:

> *Oh, the depth of the riches both of the wisdom and knowledge of God! How unsearchable are His judgments and His ways past finding out! "For who has known the mind of the* LORD*? Or who has become His counselor?" "Or who has first given to Him and it shall be repaid to him?" For of Him and through Him and to Him are all things, to whom be glory forever. Amen. (Rom. 11:33–36 NKJV)*

Pulling It All Together . . .

- Israel's rejection of Christ was actually a *good* thing, in that it caused God to extend salvation to the Gentiles as well.

- Metaphorically, the Gentiles have been "grafted in" as branches to the root, which is the Nation of Israel.

- Thus, Salvation is for all, but only through faith and not by works. Nonetheless, Paul was passionate about his desire to help his Jewish brethren believe in Christ.

RIGHTEOUSNESS IN DAILY LIVING

6

ROMANS 12:1–15:13

Before We Begin . . .

This section of Romans contains the well-known quote from Paul, to "present your bodies as a living sacrifice to God." What does this mean to you?

This section of Romans also contains Paul's admonition to "let every soul be subject to the governing authorities," and "there is no authority except from God, and the authorities that exist are appointed by God." Considering recent history especially, how do you feel about this message from Paul? In what context did he offer it? Does it always apply, in all times and places?

ROMANS CHAPTER 12

This chapter of Romans begins with another of those memorable passages that help to bring so much of Paul's letters to life. Rather than filling in blanks, read the two verses below and then answer the questions that follow:

> *I beseech you therefore, brethren, by the mercies of God, that you present your bodies a living sacrifice, holy, acceptable to God, which is your reasonable service. And do not be conformed to this world, but be transformed by the renewing of your mind, that you may prove what is that good and acceptable and perfect will of God. (Rom. 12:1–2 NKJV)*

What did Paul tell us is our "reasonable service"?

What are we NOT to be conformed to? What should transform us?

What did Paul say is the reason for which we should be transformed?

SERVE GOD WITH SPIRITUAL GIFTS

In verse 3, how did Paul tell us we ought not to think of ourselves? How should we think of ourselves?

Verses 4–8 contain another of those "glorious lessons" that Paul delighted in teaching. In your own words, can you summarize this message? How was Paul telling us we should interact with each other? What did he have to say about the relative value of each of us? What can we all contribute to the well-being of other believers?

With reference to verse 6 in the selection you have just written about, it's important to understand that the word "prophecy" does not necessarily refer to a message about future events. Old Testament prophets were men and women who essentially "spoke forth" for God; they were under His influence and they said what He wanted them to say. Thus, a prophet could also be called a teacher, one who speaks forth the truth concerning the Word of God whether that truth involves past, present, or future events.

BEHAVE LIKE A CHRISTIAN

What did Paul say that love should be without, in verse 9?

What should we abhor? What should we cling to?

In verses 12–21, Paul continued the list he had already started and gave us at least *18 additional things that we should do (not just "be," but* do*!). In the spaces below, see how many of those 18 things you can list.*

1.   2.

3.   4.

5.   6.

7.   8.

9.   10.

11.   12.

13.   14.

15.   16.

17.   18.

ROMANS CHAPTER 13

SUBMIT TO GOVERNMENT

The first few verses of this chapter have caused some concern among believers, who interpret Paul's instructions to mean that all authorities are individually appointed by God. This is not what Paul was saying in verse 1; on the contrary, most scholars establish the all-important *context* of Paul's remarks in one of two ways.

First, some scholars look at these verses within a very *large* context and believe that Paul was simply acknowledging that the whole concept of human government was established by God in Genesis 9:6, after the Flood, when God said, "Whoever sheds man's blood, by man his blood shall be shed." In other words, God ordained the concept of government by our peers, but He did not necessarily appoint the individuals who function within it. Truly, this is a "big concept" approach.

Second, other scholars look at these verses within a somewhat *smaller* context and believe that Paul was specifically addressing the situation faced by the Gentile believers within the Roman congregation. Regardless of how strongly they believed in Jesus Christ they were still outsiders meeting with Jews in a Jewish synagogue, and thus they were subject to any number of rules and provisions that they might have found at least a little bit irritating, perplexing, or even onerous. The men who wrote those rules, of course, were the members of the Sanhedrin (which, as mentioned elsewhere in this study guide, some scholars believe Paul himself would have been in line to lead had he not chosen to believe that Christ was the true Messiah) and/or the individual Jewish leaders of each synagogue. This view of the situation seems slightly more credible, because Paul certainly could have believed that the members of the Sanhedrin were appointed by God and were doing His business, and likewise with other Jewish religious leaders as well.

In addition, all the other comments Paul made with regard to governing authorities track a lot better when applied to religious leaders rather than with civil authorities. Certainly it would have been difficult for Paul to assert that the pagan Romans were appointed by God to kill, conquer, and oppress his own people. They did this in any number of ways prior to AD 70, at which time they declared open season, destroyed the Jewish temple, killed as many Jews as they could, and drove the rest out of Jerusalem.

With all that in mind, read chapter 13 and answer the following questions.

In verse 1, Paul said that the governing authorities were appointed by whom?

If someone resists any such authority, who, in effect, are they therefore resisting?

What did Paul mean in verse 3, when he said that "rulers are not a terror to good works, but to evil"? Do you believe this is an accurate statement?

What two reasons for being subject to the authorities did Paul give in verse 5? Can you express these two reasons in modern language?

Do you remember a quotation from Jesus, that paralleled what Paul said in verse 7? If so, write it in as you remember it in the space below. (Hint: Think Matthew 22:21.)

LOVE YOUR NEIGHBOR

This section of chapter 13 includes an extremely brief discussion of the law, summarized by Paul's statement in verse 9. How did Paul express this summary?

What are the five commandments that Paul referenced, leading up to verse 9?

What did Paul say that loves does not do, in verse 10?

Chapter 13 concludes with the following four verses. Fill in the blanks to see how Paul brought this chapter to a close.

> *And do this, knowing the _____, that now it is high time to awake out of _____; for now our _____ is nearer than when we first believed. The night is far spent, the day is at hand. Therefore let us cast off the works of _____, and let us put on the _____ of light. Let us walk properly, as in the day, not in _____ and drunkenness, not in _____ and lust, not in strife and envy. But put on the Lord Jesus Christ, and make no provision for the flesh, to fulfill its lusts. (Rom. 13:11–14 NKJV)*

ROMANS CHAPTER 14

THE LAW OF LIBERTY AND THE LAW OF LOVE

Before studying chapter 14, please read the two sidebars in this chapter, entitled "Holy Days and Holy Foods" and "Why Was Paul Still Talking about 'Clean' and 'Unclean' Foods?" Otherwise, without that perspective, it is extremely difficult to fully understand some of Paul's comments in the following verses. Please continue with the questions below, once you have read those two passages to help give you a historical context.

In verse 1, what did Paul say we are to do with respect to one who is "weak in the faith"?

What are we not to do?

What do you believe Paul meant by "doubtful things"?

What did Paul mean, in verse 2, when he spoke of "he who is weak eats only vegetables"? Is eating only vegetables a sign of weakness, or did Paul have something else in mind here?

Read verse 3, then write down your interpretation of what Paul meant by all this talk about "eating" and "judging." What do you know about the Jewish dietary laws and customs that would help explain Paul's meaning? What do you also know about the vast gulf in understanding between Jews and Gentiles on these subjects, especially in ancient times?

Verses 3b–4 also help draw this short section together. In the "master/servant" dialogue, what was Paul's main point?

Who do you think he might have been referring to by the word "master"? Why do you think so?

What did Paul say, in verse 4, that God is able to do for each of His servants?

In verses 5–8, Paul offered his own take on several matters that have brought honest differences in opinion, more than once, between sincere believers in Christ. Using the concept of a day considered holy unto the Lord, Paul took a very lofty (some might say radical!) approach. His concern was not whether some men or women might consider one day—or one meal or one food—more important than another, but that all be fully convinced in their own minds that God is directing them, for each believer's individual accountability to God is ultimately the most important consideration.

In that context, what did Paul say in verse 8? That we live and die to whom?

In verses 9–11, Paul added the theological underpinnings to what he had just said. What is your take on what he said in these verses? What did he say is truly most important? What did he say that we, as believers, should not *be doing? And, most important of all, where and by whom did he say that we shall all be judged?*

HOLY DAYS AND HOLY FOODS

The 14th chapter of Romans, beginning especially with verse 14 and extending through verse 23, contains a number of statements that can be almost mystifying if we do not understand the historical context. First of all, remember that Paul is addressing three groups of people simultaneously: (1) Jews who have already accepted Christ as their Messiah; (2) Jews who have rejected Him but are, in many cases, still receptive and might yet be convinced that He is who He said He is, if they are not grossly affronted and driven away; and (3) Gentiles from outside the Jewish community who have come to faith in Christ but have no understanding of Jewish customs and traditions. Indeed, many of these Gentiles came directly to belief in Christ from pagan backgrounds.

Second, do not assume that, when Paul mentioned "days that some considered holy while others did not," he was talking about the Sabbath. Recall, again, that Paul was a Jew from birth, as were many of the recipients of his letter. To them the Sabbath was the seventh day, just as it had always been since the moment God decreed it so in Genesis 2:2–3. However, all Jewish congregations of that era also had certain *halakha*, or "observance customs," or "ways in which they observed *Torah*," which were considered almost holy in their application. Many of these *halakha* did not change down through the generations; others did, but the goal was always the same—to help each person follow *Torah* as closely as he was able. Thus, the *halakha* of the Roman Jews undoubtedly included certain days on which they fasted together, and other days on which they feasted together and celebrated both their separate and their joint relationships with God.

But those particular holy days were not commanded by God, and thus they certainly would *not* be equally holy to Gentiles from outside the Jewish community.

Third, Paul was also not talking about kosher foods, for this, too, was not a negotiable issue for the Jews in the Roman congregation. On the other hand, even

HOLY DAYS AND HOLY FOODS (CONT.)

though (for example) the cow was considered a "clean" animal, the kosher laws of that era (and of modern times, too) required that the blood of a cow be handled in a certain way when the animal was slaughtered. If this did not happen, the animal was then considered spiritually unclean and could not knowingly be eaten by a devout Jew. Thus the Jewish members of the Roman congregation were very wary of eating with the Gentile members, for they had no way of knowing for sure how any meat brought by a Gentile had been prepared—or, whether it had first been offered to an idol. And they were far more willing to eat nothing than they were to take a chance.

In other words, what Paul was saying here had nothing to do with the clear commandments God gave to the children of Israel, in His Word, about (1) keeping the Sabbath and (2) observing what have come to be known as the *kashrut* or "kosher laws," with respect to clean and unclean animals. These are never to be compromised.

In more modern terms, we might suggest that Paul was telling the Romans not to get hung up on customs and traditions that were not salvation issues. As Christ Himself demonstrated when He went to the temple in Jerusalem to celebrate Hanukkah (i.e., the Feast of Dedication in John 10:21–23), as long as the traditions of Jews and Gentiles alike did not hinder other members of the congregation from developing close, personal, obedient relationships with God, Paul had no problem with them.

Also, coming at this from the other direction, Paul was saying that he would have little objection to any traditions the Gentiles might bring into the mix with them as well, as long as they did not directly oppose or negate God's commandments. A good example, though it was not current in biblical times, would be the pagan Yule tree tradition that modern Christians associate with Christmas . . . but which has absolutely nothing to do with the birth of Christ. Or, the pagan-based Easter bunny and baby chicken traditions many Christians still observe at the commemoration of Jesus' Resurrection.

"Make sure you have gas in the tank and oil in the engine," said Paul. "If you take care of those things—and keep the engine tuned up as well—you can run the race whether your seat covers are made of leather, plastic, or geranium blossoms."

To bring this short section to a close, fill in the blanks in the following passage.

So then each of us shall give account of himself to _____. Therefore let us not _____ one another anymore, but rather resolve this, not to put a _____ block or a cause to fall in our _____ way. (Rom. 14:12–13 NKJV)

The Law of Love

In verse 14, what did Paul say about "unclean" things?

What advice did Paul therefore give us, in verses 15–18? Can you put all this in your own words? What did he specifically say we should not *do?*

Do the same with verses 19–23. What do you think Paul was saying in these verses? Can you put it into your own words?

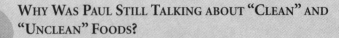

WHY WAS PAUL STILL TALKING ABOUT "CLEAN" AND "UNCLEAN" FOODS?

Why was Paul still bringing up the issue of clean and unclean foods? Why, indeed, does it come up even today?

Let's look at a bit of biblical history. Even before God explained to Moses, in the eleventh chapter of Leviticus, which foods were clean and unclean—and therefore allowed or forbidden for the Jews to eat—the distinction had already been made. How else would Noah have known which animals were clean and unclean when he loaded the ark? Or, which ones to sacrifice in gratitude and worship of God when dry land appeared again? By the time the children of Israel got to Mount Sinai, God was simply codifying and clarifying what He had already made known to their ancestors.

But why? Why did God declare certain foods unclean? Why was (is) it okay to eat a cow but not a pig? Why a bass or a tuna but not a shrimp or an eel?

Many commentators down through the centuries, Christian and otherwise, have tried to make human sense out of the kosher laws—to justify or nullify them, once for all, according to some system of human logic that would render them fully understandable by human standards. But in truth it cannot be done. The only way to comprehend the kosher laws is to look at them from God's perspective. Even so, we cannot know the mind of God; the best we can do is to postulate some possibilities.

Perhaps the kosher laws were given by God to the ancient Jews to . . .

1. Set them apart from the pagan tribes surrounding them and make them special to Him alone. For example, he told them not to "boil a young goat in its mother's milk" (Deut. 14:21) because this was a pagan practice that He considered detestable.

2. Teach them self-discipline.

3. Keep thoughts of God in their minds all the time, in obvious accord with the well-known *Shema* of Deuteronomy 6:4–9, in which He also commanded them to keep His words ever before them, even writing them on the doorposts of their homes. (This, incidentally, is a custom modern Jews still observe, by inserting small passages of Scripture into small, decorative boxes made of metal, ceramic, or wood—known as *mezzuzot*—which are then fastened to front door jambs and touched each time a person enters or leaves the house.)

4. Give them an opportunity to show God that they loved Him, by demonstrating their willing obedience on a constant, daily basis.

> **WHY WAS PAUL STILL TALKING ABOUT "CLEAN" AND "UNCLEAN" FOODS? (CONT.)**
>
> Some scholars have also suggested that God gave the Jews the kosher laws to preserve their health. Indeed, modern science tells us that goat meat is far more healthful for human consumption than the meat of pigs. But to the Jews, this argument seems incomplete and questionable at best, for it would remove all suggestion of any spiritual reasons for God's decree. The health benefits were strictly that . . . benefits. But they were not the reason.

ROMANS CHAPTER 15

In verse 1, Paul said that the strong "ought to bear with the scruples of the weak." In this case the word "scruples" could also be translated as "failings" or "lack of strong principles." In other words, those who are strong in their faith, and in their understanding of godly things, need to be supportive of those who are not. Not judgmental, not condemnatory, not skeptical or dismissive, but supportive even to the point of looking ahead to good results and focusing on them, rather than concentrating on the present situation (whatever that might be) and bemoaning what's directly in front of us.

This is truly a simplified summary, or introduction, to chapter 15. However, once again we have to recognize how difficult it can be to take one verse at a time from Paul's writings and pull out ultimate meaning from it. The ancient Hebrews believed that all Scriptures could be understood only in context, meaning that they would often go a minimum of one chapter before and one chapter behind any verse they wished to concentrate on. To them, that was considered appropriate context, and we would often do well to emulate that example.

In any case, it's now your turn! Please read Romans 15:1–12, but concentrate on verses 1–9, because the remaining verses are quotations from the Old Testament, used by Paul to illustrate what he had just said. Then do your best to recap these verses in the space provided.

What was Paul trying to convey here?

How does this message apply to your daily life?

To that of your church? To that of all *Christians, all over the world?*

Finally, even though we still have several verses to go in chapters 15 and 16, this section of chapter 15 ends with a typical Pauline benediction: "Now may the God of hope fill you with all joy and peace in believing, that you may abound in hope by the power of the Holy Spirit" (Rom. 15:13 NKJV).

PULLING IT ALL TOGETHER . . .

In this portion of Romans Paul tells us . . .

• That we should lead transformed lives once we accept salvation through Christ.

• That we should serve God with all of our spiritual gifts.

• That we should obey the duly constituted civil authorities.

• That we should love our neighbors.

• That we should observe both the law of liberty and the law of love, by balancing our liberty against our love and concern for others, making sure that by exercising our rights we do not lead others astray.

• That we should bear each other's burdens and glorify God in all that we do.

7 | FINAL CONSIDERATIONS

ROMANS 15:14–16:27

Before We Begin ...

What is your impression of Paul, with respect to how he characterizes himself? Does he seem arrogant and proud, humble and subdued, or what else?

How do you feel about avoiding people who could have a negative influence on your life? Is this a "Christian" thing to do?

All of Paul's letters end with clearly identifiable closing remarks. Most often these contain a number of greetings to individual friends within the community to which he was writing, plus extra, often quite specific words of personal advice and encouragement. The book of Romans is no exception, but here his closing remarks are more extensive than they are anywhere else. Most scholars attribute Paul's unusual verbosity in these concluding verses to three possible reasons.

First, because Paul had never visited Rome, he might have been extra careful to end with praise for the people he had never met, to be absolutely sure that they would not misunderstand either his intent or his high regard for what they had already accomplished, all virtually on their own (but with the help of the Holy Spirit, of course!). Second, Paul undoubtedly wanted to establish personal relationships with members of the congregation by giving them plenty of reason to trust his motives and to respond to him personally, if they so desired. Third, as Paul made clear, he planned to visit Rome in person as soon as possible, and he certainly would have wanted to prepare the way.

Romans Chapter 15:14–27

Starting with verse 14, to get a feel for how Paul pursued the previous objectives, please answer the following questions.

In verse 14, what did Paul say he was "confident concerning"?

What is the main point of verses 15–16? What did Paul acknowledge that he had done in his letter to the Romans, and why did he say that he had done it?

In verses 17–19, why did Paul say that he had reason to glory? In what? What had he personally done, which qualified him to speak to them as he had?

What is your understanding of verses 20–21? Was Paul proclaiming himself a leader or a follower?

PAUL'S PLAN TO VISIT ROME

Why did Paul say, in verse 22, that he had been hindered from going to Rome? What does the word "hindered" refer to?

Where did Paul say, in verse 24, that he would eventually be going, beyond Rome?

Given Paul's additional comments in verse 24, what did he plan to do, on that journey, with respect to Rome? And what did he hope to gain from his friends in Rome?

In verses 25–26, where did Paul say he must go first? From where? Why?

Fill in the blanks in the passage below, to see how Paul ended this chapter.

> *Now I beg you, _____, through the Lord Jesus Christ, and through the love of the Spirit, that you strive together with me in _____ to God for me, that I may be delivered from those in _____ who do not believe, and that my service for _____ may be acceptable to the _____, that I may come to you with joy by the will of God, and may be _____ together with you. Now the God of _____ be with you all. Amen. (Rom. 15:30–33 NKJV)*

ROMANS CHAPTER 16

FINAL COMMENDATIONS AND GREETINGS

In verses 1–16, Paul referred to at least twenty-five people by name, to whom he extended personal greetings and commendations. In the table on the following page, you will find listed most of what he said about each of these people. No need to fill in any blanks; just look through the table to get a good sense of how Paul felt about various people and how careful and respectful he was in talking about them.

Phoebe	who is a servant of the church in Cenchrea, that you may receive her in the Lord in a manner worthy of the saints, and assist her in whatever business she has need of you; for indeed she has been a helper of many and of myself also
Priscilla and Aquila	my fellow workers in Christ Jesus, who risked their own necks for my life, to whom not only I give thanks, but also all the churches of the Gentiles. Likewise greet the church that is in their house
Epaenetus	who is the firstfruits of Achaia to Christ
Mary	who labored much for us
Andronicus and Junia	my countrymen and my fellow prisoners, who are of note among the apostles, who also were in Christ before me
Amplias	my beloved in the Lord
Urbanus	our fellow worker in Christ
Stachys	my beloved
Apelles	approved in Christ
Herodion	my countryman
Tryphena and Tryphosa	who have labored in the Lord
Persis	who labored much in the Lord
Rufus	chosen in the Lord, and [greet] his mother and mine
Asyncritus, Phlegon, Hermas, Patrobas, Hermes	and the brethren who are with them
Philologus and Julia, Nereus and his sister, and Olympas	and all the saints who are with them

AVOID DIVISIVE PERSONS

Just before Paul included final greetings from his own friends, at his own end of the conversation, he added one or two final admonitions to the Romans, in verses 17–20.

Who does Paul say that the brethren to whom he is writing should avoid? Why?

PAUL AND HIS FRIENDS

Paul's letter to the Romans ended with a long section in which Paul sent greetings to various people. The total number of words he devoted to personal greetings and commendations, in fact, amounts to nearly 10% of the total of all the words in the letter, which seems unusually high.

On the other hand, recall that Paul was a highly respected rabbi and might well have been next in line to head the Sanhedrin, had he not come to believe in Jesus Christ as the true Jewish Messiah. Given his background, it's not the least bit surprising that he would know a lot of people within the Jewish community. And given his mission as an emissary for Christ, it's also not the least bit surprising that he would sometimes be almost effusive in his praise and consideration for others.

The first person he mentioned was a woman named Phoebe. Because of the way Paul commends her to the Romans, many scholars believe that Phoebe might have been both the courier and the first reader of Paul's letter.

That is, she was apparently a businesswoman of some skill. Paul even asked the Romans to help her in her business affairs, if possible. Someone would have had to carry the letter from Paul and deliver it to its intended recipients. Why not Phoebe? It's certainly possible that she could have been the one who read the letter first, out loud, perhaps to several small groups of believers in Rome.

What did he say about the listed people; that is, whom do they not serve, and whom or what do they serve instead?

In verse 19, what did Paul say he wanted for his brethren in Rome?

Finally, what did he say that the "God of peace" will do to Satan?

BENEDICTION

Paul concluded with the following words—truly, a profound and heartfelt benediction to all that has gone before.

> *Now to Him who is able to establish you according to my gospel and the preaching of Jesus Christ, according to the revelation of the mystery kept secret since the world began but now made manifest, and by the prophetic Scriptures made known to all nations, according to the commandment of the everlasting God, for obedience to the faith—to God, alone wise, be glory through Jesus Christ forever. Amen. (Rom. 16:25–27 NKJV)*

And so ends the book of Romans.

PULLING IT ALL TOGETHER . . .

• Paul explained that he planned to visit the Roman congregation as soon as he could, on his way from Jerusalem to Spain.

• He commended and personally greeted a large number of people in the Roman congregation, starting with Phoebe, Priscilla and Aquila, and ending with Philologus and Julia, Nereus, and Olympas.

• He told the Romans to avoid divisive people—those who serve themselves and not Christ.

• He added a number of personal greetings from his own friends and fellow workers.

• Paul concluded the book of Romans with a powerful benediction.

COMING TO A CLOSE

By the time most readers finish the book of Romans, they find themselves totally in awe of the apostle Paul and the huge message he was able—through the help of the Holy Spirit—to distill into such a small space. Indeed, more than one person has finished Romans, turned back to the first page, and started all over again on the same day!

For most people, this does not happen because they read Romans and were hopelessly confused, but because they felt so "filled up" and energized by the things Paul had to say, they wanted to make sure they hadn't missed anything. So, before you leave the book of Romans to study other parts of the Bible, check yourself out via the following quiz.

What is the gospel (i.e., the "Good News") of Jesus Christ? Can you put it into one or two sentences?

Why do people need the gospel? And more important, why do YOU need it?

How can unholy sinners be justified by a Holy God? What provision does God now make for that? What provision did He make in ancient times, before the time of Christ?

What portion of what Paul called "the law" (meaning all that's contained in the first five books of the Bible) are we still expected to keep? For example, what about the Ten Commandments?

What portion are we not expected to keep?

What provision does God make for us, so that we can live what He will consider holy lives?

Can anything that Paul taught in Romans be interpreted to encourage intentional sin?

Is there anything in Paul's message to suggest that God has changed His mind in any way with regard to His chosen people, the Jews? For example, has He broken His covenant with the Jews by offering the gospel to the Gentiles?

Do you believe that God is even capable *of breaking a covenant? Why, or why not?*

If the answers to any of these questions are unclear to you, please go back and reread the sections in Romans that apply. Beyond that, if your own private study still leaves you with questions, get your hands on a good commentary, a Bible handbook, or any one of the hundreds of books now available to help you understand the true meaning of the book of Romans.

As you well know by now, Romans is surely as central to the fundamental doctrines of Christianity as any book in the Bible. Do not stop studying it now that you've completed this guide—come back again and again.

God always rewards those who study His Word . . . and the book of Romans is one of the preeminent proofs of this long-established truth.

HOW TO BUILD YOUR
REFERENCE LIBRARY

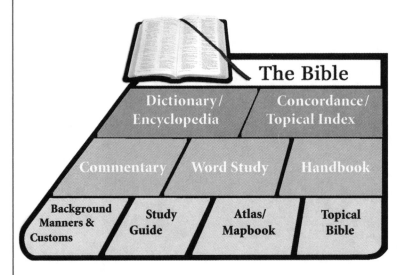

GREAT RESOURCES FOR BUILDING YOUR REFERENCE LIBRARY

DICTIONARIES AND ENCYCLOPEDIAS

All About the Bible: The Ultimate A-to-Z® Illustrated Guide to the Key People, Places, and Things

Every Man in the Bible by Larry Richards

Every Woman in the Bible by Larry Richards and Sue Richards

Nelson's Compact Bible Dictionary

Nelson's Illustrated Encyclopedia of the Bible

Nelson's New Illustrated Bible Dictionary

Nelson's Student Bible Dictionary

So That's What It Means! The Ultimate A-to-Z Resource by Don Campbell, Wendell Johnston, John Walvoord, and John Witmer

Vine's Complete Expository Dictionary of Old and New Testament Words by W. E. Vine and Merrill F. Unger

CONCORDANCES AND TOPICAL INDEXES

Nelson's Quick Reference Bible Concordance by Ronald F. Youngblood

The New Strong's Exhaustive Concordance of the Bible by James Strong

COMMENTARIES

Believer's Bible Commentary by William MacDonald

Matthew Henry's Concise Commentary on the Whole Bible by Matthew Henry

The MacArthur Bible Commentary by John MacArthur

Nelson's New Illustrated Bible Commentary

Thru the Bible series by J. Vernon McGee

HANDBOOKS

Nelson's Compact Bible Handbook

Nelson's Complete Book of Bible Maps and Charts

Nelson's Illustrated Bible Handbook

Nelson's New Illustrated Bible Manners and Customs by Howard F. Vos

With the Word: The Chapter-by-Chapter Bible Handbook by Warren W. Wiersbe

For more great resources, please visit *www.thomasnelson.com.*

NELSON IMPACT™ STUDY GUIDES

NELSON IMPACT
A Division of Thomas Nelson Publishers
Since 1798

www.thomasnelson.com

The Finest Study Bible EVER!

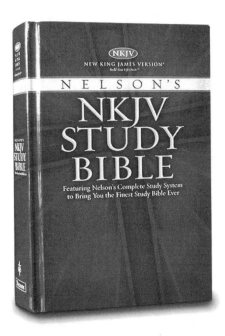

Nelson's NKJV Study Bible helps you understand, apply and
grow in a life-long journey through God's Word.

    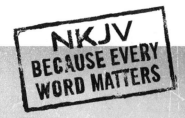

NELSON BIBLES
A Division of Thomas Nelson Publishers
Since 1798

NEW KING JAMES VERSION®
Build Your Life On It.™

NELSON IMPACT
A Division of Thomas Nelson Publishers
Since 1798

The Nelson Impact Team is here to answer your questions
and suggestions as to how we can create more resources
that benefit you, your family, and your community.

Contact us at Impact@thomasnelson.com